THE GOSPEL OF RISK AND ITS ENEMIES

Fundamentalism and Liberalism

M.H. DAVIS

Copyright © 2010 M H Davis

The moral right of the author has been asserted.

Scripture quotations taken from the HOLY BIBLE, NEW INTERNATIONAL VERSION.
Copyright © 1973, 1978, 1984 by International Bible Society.
Used by permission of Hodder & Stoughton Publishers, A member of the Hachette Livre UK Group.
All rights reserved.
"NIV" is a registered trademark of International Bible Society.
UK trademark number 1448790.

Apart from any fair dealing for the purposes of research or private study, or criticism or review, as permitted under the Copyright, Designs and Patents Act 1988, this publication may only be reproduced, stored or transmitted, in any form or by any means, with the prior permission in writing of the publishers, or in the case of reprographic reproduction in accordance with the terms of licences issued by the Copyright Licensing Agency. Enquiries concerning reproduction outside those terms should be sent to the publishers.

Matador
5 Weir Road
Kibworth Beauchamp
Leicester LE8 0LQ, UK
Tel: (+44) 116 279 2299
Email: books@troubador.co.uk
Web: www.troubador.co.uk/matador

ISBN 978-1848762-718

A Cataloguing-in-Publication (CIP) catalogue record for this book is available from the British Library.

Typeset in 11pt Palatino by Troubador Publishing Ltd, Leicester, UK
Printed in Great Britain by the MPG Books Group, Bodmin and King's Lynn

Matador is an imprint of Troubador Publishing Ltd

To gain eternity without risking anything
is impossible.
Soren Kierkegaard, Journals

CONTENTS

INTRODUCTION   vii

1 CHRISTIAN FUNDAMENTALIST CONFORMISM   1

2 CHRISTIAN LIBERAL CONFORMISM   31

3 FAILURE OF FUNDAMENTALISM
   AND LIBERALISM   58

4 THE GOSPEL OF RISK   82

CONCLUSION: RISK, GROWTH AND MATURITY   118

NOTES   155

INTRODUCTION

There has only ever been one authentic Christian gospel: the gospel of risk. First and foremost it is the gospel of Jesus Christ, the Messiah, the crucified and risen Saviour of the world, who as soon as he engaged on his public ministry was in danger physically, mentally and spiritually from all the evil forces of the world. Throughout Jesus of Nazareth's ministry, despite the increasing signs of mounting opposition, he never eschewed the risk-ridden pathway which always lay before him. Therefore his gospel was always the gospel of risk, for its 'enunciation' (proclaiming) and its 'doing' (works) continually invoked misunderstanding, hatred and condemnation in his enemies. The gospel of risk's great historic culmination was and is the cross; the sudden apparent ending of Christ's ministry route with his nailing to a wooden beam in a putrid place reserved for the execution of criminals outside the city walls.

All the great apostles and those like-minded spirits who followed them in the opening centuries of the early Church, maintained the authenticity of the gospel of risk. In most part they maintained it in the way of the Saviour; at the cost of their very lives. Since the 'heady' era of early Christianity the history of Christ's church on earth has been subject to much development, fluctuation and to much internal division with resultant splintering into various segmented factions. Despite the often abandonment of the gospel of risk by various church leaders and cleric practitioners there has always been down the succeeding ages, great figures of resolute conscience who have staked all to uphold Christ's authentic gospel. This, the true gospel, not the gospel of self-satisfaction, self-congratulation or self-comfort, but the gospel enshrined in Christ's words:

> "If anyone would come after me, he must deny himself and take up his cross and follow me. For whoever wants to save his life will lose it, but whoever loses his life for me will find it". (1)

Take away these words and one has immediately lost the core of Christianity. And it is when the Church – or its various segments of denominations – forgets or chooses to forget these words that Christianity is manifested in a false light. The gospel of risk is a gospel which cannot bypass or evade suffering. There is indeed experience of joy and peace for those who are re-birthed in Christ, but there is also the demand for self-sacrifice, for renunciation of the old Adam-self. And this is precisely where the cost and pain lies. A Christianity without a cost to its adherents is mere chicanery. We do well to remember J.B. Phillips' warning:

> "Christianity is full of joy, but it is not a joy-ride".(2)

And in fact all in the true line of great Christian reformers, revivalists and thinkers have always insisted on this point of view. Thus we have for instance, Martin Luther's re-centring of theology on the cross, with its emphasis weighted on the costliness of the salvation wrought by Christ ; we have John Wesley often putting himself at considerable personal risk in preaching the gospel outside the relative safety of church walls; and a thinker such as Soren Kierkegaard who chose the bitter task of an isolated prophet riding against the grain of a complacent middle class Christendom.

Throughout the centuries there has always been the danger for Christians of all persuasions and de-nominations of falling into the cosy trap of conformity. What I am concerned about in this book is precisely this danger with reference to contemporary Christianity. But it is a danger which I believe is manifest on two quite different fronts. For this reason the problem is at once more exacting, requiring as it were two separate responses which deal specifically with each of these forms of Christian conformity. However, the capital difficulty lies in the fact that these two threats to the pursual of the authentic gospel, namely contemporary Christian fundamentalism and Christian liberalism, are both at loggerheads with one another. In other words, fundamentalists and liberals regard each other, if not quite as deadly foes, at least as very dangerously misguided opponents. Further, none of those who make up the members of these two ism's would regard themselves as complacent conformists. In fact they would feel absolutely insulted to be viewed in such a manner! For on the contrary, both the fundamentalists and liberals regard themselves as being radical in what they do. In most cases they genuinely believe that they are promoting Christianity in the best possible way.

My intention in this book is to give an overview of the reasons why the fundamentalists and liberalist groupings of the western Christian Church tend to think along their respective thought lines and to put forward the case that despite having some very positive aspects, they both end up in the deadlock of complacency and conformity – albeit often unknowingly to the adherents. It must also be added here that this book is examining fundamentalism and liberalism in terms of Protestantism rather than Catholicism. Within the latter it is reasonably clear that there are movements or tendencies which to some extent mirror Protestantism's conservative and liberal extremist groups. There are Catholic lay thinkers and theologians who are liberal to the extent of adopting a more ecumenical approach; who also possess an understanding which acknowledges such fields for example, as psychoanalysis, and who evince a deeper awareness of the challenges of the post-modern age with its massive western consumerism and the appalling poverty and oppression experienced by 'third world' peoples. But on the main, most of such 'liberal' Catholics would not seriously question the central tenets of their Christian faith. It is the nature of the great difference between Catholicism and Protestantism, that generally speaking, once a Catholic reaches the point of being unable to accept the basic doctrines of Christianity (such as the Virgin Birth and the Resurrection) he or she is a Catholic no longer; whereas a Protestant who reaches the same point can still very easily continue as a Protestant by switching to another more accommodating grouping such as the Quakers or Unitarians. On the other hand, there are some Catholics whose fundamentalist attitude very much parallels their Protestant counterparts; they have no truck with ecumenicalism or interfaith dialogue; they adhere to a pessimistic end-times view, and hold hard-line views on such issues as abortion, homosexuality and euthanasia. However, I would suggest that these type of attitudes are to some extent inherent in the inbuilt conservatism of Catholicism, and I do not regard them as forming – at least in the west – a movement matching the significance of the fundamentalist Protestant churches.

Granted then that this study will be concerned with Protestantism, it is now essential before one can go on any further to make at least some tentative definitions of what is meant by fundamentalism and liberalism with regard to contemporary twenty-first century western Christianity. It is not my intention here to attempt any wide-scale examination of fundamentalism as a historical-socio or psychological phenomenon. The term 'liberalism' (as I shall use it in the following pages) will be applicable and restricted to denoting liberalism's influential presence in western Protestantism. (Obviously, the wider sense of 'liberalism' would include as well as religion the fields of philosophy, economics, politics and education). I shall be looking broadly at liberal Protestantism's current basis and influence, and therefore it will not be my purpose to attempt a full-scale critique of the involved historical developments of liberal theology.

Thus, my object will be to try and evaluate what I take to be the particularly dominating, contemporary characteristics, or better, mentalities, of fundamentalist and liberalist Christian extrapolations and to establish their relationship to what I consider to be the authentic gospel of risk.

Firstly, then, what is contemporary Christian fundamentalism? In a nutshell it is primarily a resolutely literalist belief in the Bible, which thereby downgrades God and truth into the sphere of materialism. I would submit that this unswerving, idolatrous view, which makes the Bible into a kind of cheap answer-book to all life's problems and mysteries, is the fundamentalist's bedrock position from which all else stems. It ought perhaps be added here that Pentecostalism *per se* should not necessarily be seen as synonymous with fundamentalism as it is outlined above. Pentecostalism as a movement refers primarily not to a set of theological attitudes but rather to a particular 'releasing' way or style of worship, (being based upon a re-affirmation of the Holy Spirit's power of infusing Christians with awareness of the special charismatic gifts such as tongues and healing). As such, Pentecostal churches can, like other denominations, evince either broad-minded or more narrow-minded attitudes depending on the mentalities involved of those who lead and partake in the worship. Though it is of course true that Pentecostalism, because of its essentially vitalist approach does have strong anti-intellectual tendencies which particularly render it susceptible to the fundamentalist attitude and mentality. However, it would be both unfair and clumsy to directly equate Pentecostalism with fundamentalism as it is clear that the latter cuts across a variety of denominations which include even some episcopalian churches.

Secondly, what might serve as an initial core definition of contemporary Christian liberalism? I would suggest that the concept of human autonomy is absolutely central, and that it is autonomy with regard to the individual being absolutely free to pursue his or her own agenda in terms of interpreting and practising belief. Again, what is to be immediately noted is that by exclusively focusing on independence rather than dependence, Protestant liberalism lays itself open to self-idolatry.

The above are of course both merely basic preliminary definitions which in the following chapters I will be attempting to substantially enlarge upon. I have entitled this book: The Gospel of Risk and its Enemies, and have perceived the foremost enemies as being what I have just now roughly defined as Christian fundamentalism and Christian liberalism. However, I must again stress that these ism's are very broad umbrellas indeed. What I do not want to suggest is that fundamentalism *per se* or liberalism *per se* are both totally flawed extrapolations of Christianity. It is all too easy to condemn in a cavalier, absolutist way, and this book is not intended as merely a kind of double witch hunt. For a start, the complexity of human beings, their motivations and thought-patterns does not warrant any such easy blanket dismissals. Just as the generally used political and cultural terms, "conservative" and "liberal," are tended to be used in a rather simplistic either-or way to imply on the one hand narrowness of outlook and on the other, width of outlook, so too can fundamentalism and liberalism be crudely invoked in the same reductive fashion. I must repeat that it is not my intention to merely condemn. There is no reason why one should not try and discover and appreciate what is valuable and significant within these 'isms. Why does one in fact become critical of such movements? The answer must be that because of their extremist tendencies one feels that such movements are either veering into heresy (liberalism) or into a regressive attitude of anti-intellectualism (fundamentalism).

One becomes critical of these movements not necessarily because of their starting points, but rather because they invariably go beyond a certain point – they pass the twin points of balanced judgement and religious humility. That is to say they go too far; the proponents of these 'isms reach the point where they make all sorts of overblown and wholly opinionated statements. The extreme liberalist will assert that all western Christian theology is nothing but the remnants of some outmoded form of religious colonialism and the extreme fundamentalist will declare that if you don't believe in the literal Garden of Eden with its talking snake, you can't be a true Christian.

But aside from these gross statements which cannot possibly be substantiated in any meaningful way, there are still certain aspects within both fundamentalist and liberalist Christianity which are worth taking note of. Why in fact does any movement obtain a significant degree of popularity? Why, for instance were the Gnostic and Arian heresies such dominating episodes in the history of Christianity? Why, because as in any significant heresy, there is contained within it a powerful element of Christian truth. Thus the positive aspect of Gnosticism centres on the striking contrast between the completeness – fullness – of God and the incompleteness, the deficiency of humankind. In the case of Arianism, the positive motivating force centred on preserving the unity and divine uniqueness of God. In both examples, we thus find the expression of valuable Christian truth. No orthodox Christian would deny these basic truths, that God, in contrast to his creatures, is both absolute plenitude and undivided divinity. However, the point is that both Gnosticism and Arianism went on far beyond these admissible Christian positions. For instance, the Gnostic denial of God becoming incarnate in human flesh and the Arian denial of Christ's divine equality with God both fall into the categories of heresy because they have moved into unbiblical positions. Thus, what contains much good is spoilt by being mixed up with the application of extremist logic. Heresy is the going too far, not necessarily the initial starting point. Given such examples, it thus becomes more evident why people are drawn into the fundamentalist and liberalist extrapolations of Christianity. The initial starting points may well be very attractive and inviting, but it is what is added onto them and the direction to where they lead which constitutes the problem. Those who get involved in the ultra fundamentalist and liberalist Christian groupings usually fail to distinguish between the wholesome and extremist elements which make up such approaches. Once one uncritically goes down these 'ism pathways everything becomes more extreme; either all who don't think in a narrow, literalistic way are 'faithless', or all who accept the central church doctrines, are out of date, bigoted puritans.

It will be my purpose in the following chapters to isolate out the good from the bad characteristics in both contemporary Christian fundamentalism and liberalism. Modern human life with all its social interactions is increasingly complex. To state this is an obvious truism. However, it needs to be often restated, precisely because the tendency of people who go down extremist religious avenues is to adopt simplistic outlooks on life. And the obvious resulting danger is a Manichaean outlook on life; truth is either-or, with no gradients in between. Just as the fundamentalist brands all those who believe in evolution as heretics, so too, does the liberalist scoff at those who believe in the doctrine of Original Sin. In the one case the fundamentalist, just because he or she doesn't understand the concept of evolution, assumes it is heretical and accordingly labels all who adhere to it as liberal (e.g. heretic). In the other case the liberalist is content to assume that all Christians who believe in the doctrine of the Fall are childish literalists. And here the corresponding failure is one of not being able to accept or realize that such a key church doctrine can be understood by enlightened non-literalist approaches.

I have already drawn attention to the broad cultural terms of conservatism and liberalism as often being used as derisory labels to be stuck on opponents. But the truth in fact is that the complexity of human social life is posited on apparently conflicting and indeed, contradictory elements. Thus there are both conservative and liberal elements mixed up in most human personalities. No one is hundred per cent conservative or liberal in their personality characteristics. There are always some areas of apparent contradiction. But further, it is appropriate that at certain times one should evince a liberal attitude, for instance, forgiveness for some personal hurt or toleration of a potentially annoying disturbance. Also, it is equally appropriate at other times to hold a conservative attitude in terms of perhaps the natural environment or defending established values which have a proven quality against dubious, new ideas and approaches. In the Christian pilgrimage, just as in all human life, there are times to be conservative just as there are times to be liberal. It is merely a question of context, as Ecclesiastes says, there is "a time to embrace and a time to refrain"(3). Human life is the interplay of various responses to the existential situation. But it is clearly extremism when one remains entrenched in absolute conservative and liberalist viewpoints. The right response at the right time makes for effective and creative human living and of course this applies to both Christians and non-Christians. Therefore in a properly balanced human life there should be a creative interaction of both conservative and liberal elements. The radicalism of the gospel is posited upon a new dynamic relationship between conservative and liberal elements juxtaposed with the truly revolutionary element of incarnate grace.

A primary aim of this book will be to make it clear why Christian fundamentalism and liberalism, in their extreme, totalistic forms, are imbalances which woefully fail to adhere to the model for fruitful human interaction set by the Saviour, Jesus Christ. I will attempt to highlight the gospel of risk's radical and authentic difference from such extrapolations. But I hope in the course of this analysis to make clear that fundamentalist and liberalist elements are not in themselves in opposition to the true gospel of risk. On the contrary, I will attempt to show how such elements are in their proper context key to Christ's gospel. What I believe needs to be brought out is on the one hand the difference between a creative rather than a destructive usage of Christian fundamentals and on the other hand the difference between a creative rather than merely a *laissez-faire* usage of Christianity's great liberalistic features. The Christian gospel – Christ's authentic gospel of risk – is primarily a gospel of creative action rather than of cut and dried theory. There is of course a rich strata of theology within it, for Christ is, after all, the supreme revelation of God, but the gospel is much more concerned about 'doing' and the quality of the act of 'living'.

Authentic Christianity is first and foremost a religion of praxis; it is about boldly proclaiming the 'good news' of God's forgiveness, and about the effectual healing of all who experience lostness in terms of body, mind and spirit. Above all, the gospel is about saving what is lost; about the salvation of men and women of all races. It is about the salvation available to be freely given to those who have lost their way. And this salvation constitutes the new 'way' which is Jesus Christ, himself. What Christ's gospel is not about is extremism, fanaticism and reductionism. Rather, his gospel is concerned with human bridge-making, wholeness and harmony; the cutting free from bondage to reductive, partisan approaches to life's rich tapestry. We cannot but not remember St. John's remembrance of Christ's wonderful statement: "I have come that they may have life, and have it to the full". (4)

And to bring in the kingdom of more abundant living, one

needs a new creative orientation towards the various modes of life. It is not a case of discarding one element for another; that is, either jettisoning beliefs in key fundamentals or beliefs in key liberalistic areas. Rather, it is a case of enlarging one's perspective and this involves a new, radical re-integration of Christian elements. One can only move nearer to any great human or spiritual truth by means of a new radical re-integration of perception. But the tragedy lies in that most men and women are inherently entrenched in their orientations and prefer to carry on as they are. History for instance, proves how hard it has been to bring in new ideas concerning science and the arts and how hard it has been to effect improvements in terms of social and political justice.

Christ's gospel is the gospel of risk because Jesus came to effect the greatest revolution of all. He came incarnate, as the Son of God, in order to show humankind the way to find forgiveness, wholeness and harmony; the way out of fear, hatred, selfishness and unforgiveness. This is truly the gospel of risk. A gospel where God in Christ is prepared to voluntarily dismantle his own divine privileges and instead to mantle himself in vulnerable human flesh; prepared even to be rejected as he comes to offer men and women entrance into his glorious kingdom:

> "He was in the world, and though the world was made through him, the world did not recognise him. He came to that which was his own, but his own did not receive him". (5)

Somewhere in-between the literalist reductionism of

fundamentalism and the clinical scepticism of liberalism is the pure gospel of risk; a gospel which preserves both the polar qualities of fervour and balanced judgement, but which also adds the sheer force of God's grace in its unrelenting work of offering healing and renewing love.

CHAPTER 1

CHRISTIAN FUNDAMENTALIST CONFORMISM

We live in a bewildering and perhaps even terrifying era of change in the western world. It is an epoch characterised by instability and rapidity of movement. Technology has the vast resources of power to make unprecedented changes at unprecedented speeds. Pastoral landscapes can, for instance, be transformed almost within days into urban conurbations of noise, pollution, crowds and repetitive greyness. Technology is continually evolving new means of production and in doing so both threatens old established modes of work, education and other forms of human interest and occupation. There is begotten the very real fear of being left behind if one doesn't adapt to these new, and in many ways, revolutionary changes to the organisation of human social life. One obvious example is the increasing need to be 'computer literate', for in virtually all jobs now (as well as in most leisure activities) information is accessed via the use of computers. Communication and business (which frequently go hand in hand) are now increasingly global. Because of the sheer rapidity and penetration of technological communication the world has shrunk from its previously forbidding vast dimensions. There now seems to be no part of the planet that the internet and modern, sophisticated human endeavour cannot reach. Thus technology has virtually broken the bounds of geography, and in a sense threatens the traditional human conception of 'space' with its aura of ultimate inviolability. In this radically, iconoclastic milieu, there is a justifiable fear that nothing is 'sacred' any longer. Time, itself, which is our human existential foundation, seems under threat, for the continuity of tradition is dislocated. The past, indeed, is a very different country. The connecting threads between past and the present generations appear to be severed; the 'new ways' in their almost contemptuous dismissal of the 'old ways', threaten to throw the baby out with the bath water. The future is uncertain. The dislocation of the past from the present via the almost demonic, helter-skelter technological changes, cuts the vital thread of continuity, which links the generations. There is indeed, considering the major threats, such as environmental exhaustion of the planet and a catastrophic nuclear war, a very real fear that there will not be a future at all. In purely human terms, our planet can no longer be considered a "world without end". From what appertains to secularist society and its relation to the future, there are no longer such things as stability and certainty. Coupled with all this is the beleaguered present, where the individual finds himself or herself bombarded with news stories highlighting the plight of the world's many war-torn and famine afflicted countries. Then on top of all this, the individual is saturated by the 'media' with triviality and useless, throwaway information.

All this must seem merely the reciting of obvious truisms about the state of much of today's western world. However, in the context of my following remarks about Christian fundamentalism it is important to be reminded again of the background canvas. Nothing springs out of a vacuum. Christian fundamentalism has of course its own key historical moments, such as the American conference held at Niagara in 1895, which outlined its essential five point fundamentalist charter. (1) However, it is the understanding of the twentieth century background of ongoing, far-reaching, revolutionary changes affecting both the superstructure and infrastructure of western societies, which is key to the answer as to why fundamentalism has become such a widespread and populist power.

It is in the context of this apparently ceaseless merry-go-round of change with all its attendant, unsettling displacements of traditional modes and codes of human social operating that Christian fundamentalism has evolved to function supremely as a religion of psychological compensation. That is to say, if this world appears now to be madly out of control, riddled with wars, greed, environmental disasters and the instability caused by continual change, Christian fundamentalism acts as a kind of psychological breast-feeding, where one can again experience like a baby, safety, security and comfort. In the face of what seems a hostile and perplexing outside world the baby can take refuge in its mother. Whereas this is, or should be, merely a stage of developmental experience in the baby, for the fundamentalist the recourse to biblical literalism with all its attendant black and whites, is nothing less than psychological regression.

And this is the first important factor of Christian fundamentalism: a massive reaction of fear to the instability of post-modern existence. Now I am well aware that the analogy with an infant breast-feeding must appear rather as an insulting slight to any Christian fundamentalist. Regression, of course implies a value judgement denoting immaturity but it can also be stating what is the case in merely a sympathetic, observational way. In one obvious sense it is a good thing to feel, safe and shielded from a world where things seem to be running amok The fearful, Hobbesian conception of non-civically organised life as "...poor, nasty, brutish and short" (2), (thus emphasising the sheer ugliness of 'natural man'), is clearly an impossible philosophy to live by. Hobbes' own answer was the pragmatic lesser evil of Leviathan. The fundamentalist shares Hobbes' basis reaction of fear to the frighteningly unstable aspects of the world which surround the individual. Of course, in Hobbes' case the fear is bound up with the thought that human beings, without any imposed socio-political constraints behave merely as selfish egos at perpetual war with one another. In the case of the Christian fundamentalist the fear is more widespread. There is indeed fear of anarchy on the raw Hobbesian human level, but also as we have noted, fear of the anarchy of change; above all, fear of changing ideas, particularly fear of new scientific and psychological conceptions of what it is to be human. But in each case safety is looked for, because both the seventeenth century Hobbes and the post-modern fundamentalists are looking for a barrier which they can erect against what they so desperately fear: namely a tidal flood waiting to engulf all that makes their life safe and secure. Thus, accepting the obvious differences of historical context and thought, the motive of preservation is key for both Hobbes and Christian fundamentalists. And in this sense one can appreciate the same archetypal compelling force which motors both these historically different, but hugely conservative reactions.

Fear. One should not belittle the fact of fear. Rather, it is important to accept that it exists and is a key, if submerged factor in all of us, whether we are Christian fundamentalists or not. The truisms I have outlined above concerning the radical instability and uncertain prospects of life on earth, affect us all. Deep down we are all afraid. No one in the end likes continual change, and no one without some modicum of intelligence can ignore the combined warning signs of devastating wars, nuclear build-ups, population explosions and ecological disasters. In this respect we are all in the same boat, and indeed, as members of the human race, created in God's image, we all face the same problems. Moreover, we are all part of the problem of sin which is the root cause of all that is awry on planet earth. Given this truth it would be proper humility for Christians of *all* persuasions to acknowledge a bond of common humanity. We are, it is important to repeat, all made in the image of God, our universal Father. We are irreparably linked together in this ongoing human drama. The problems that face the Christians who turn to fundamentalism are the same problems which face Christians who choose or search for perhaps deeper, more challenging and more enriching answers. The problems are the same; the fear, whether visible or submerged, is the same. But the mentality and attitudes which deal with the fear are of course different, and hence the entirely different responses.

The Christian fundamentalist fear, however, does not arise solely from the socio-political background. There are related psychological and intelligence factors also involved. For instance, the mark of someone who eschews intelligent debate and who has constant recourse to stock responses, is that of both psychological and rational deficiency. As I have said, fear is a reality for us all. But how as a Christian do you deal with fear? The seminal danger of fear is that it can close us up as human beings. For instance, with a person, subject or situation which we do not like it is easy to close up shop, as it were. And when a person is closed up with regard to not being prepared to adapt to say, different viewpoints and cultural perspectives, he or she is in effect withholding the social release of their full God-given humanity. They are like the fearful servant of Christ's parable, who hid the money that his master entrusted to him.(3) The servant is engulfed by a fearful attitude and rather than investing the money given him, he hides it away. The result is, of course, that the money yields no growth and the servant incurs the master's wrath. Each human being, because being born in the image of God (albeit, a sin-fractured image) has been endued with unique personal qualities. These giftings need to be shared and thus released into the world of human social interaction. But the tragic fact of the matter is that so many people bury them away in fear. They are afraid of taking these giftings out of the cupboard and risking the further growth of them in social interaction. They would rather preserve these God-given abilities as they are. And so there is sadly, so often, an embalming of what would potentially make up a full and rich, living spiritualised humanity. There is a fear in all of us of *letting go*. We all hinder our own self-development by locking up the precious gifts God has bestowed upon us at our birth.

This fear of *letting go*, is, I believe, a central psychological facet of Christian fundamentalism. If security and certainty are the overriding criteria for religious faith, then everything else will take a back-stage seat.. Holding onto what one has becomes more important than anything else. But like the fearful servant in the parable, the fundamentalist does not realize that the only real Christian way of holding onto something is paradoxically, to let go of it! Thus, Christ's mysterious words:

> "Whoever finds his life will lose it, and whoever loses his life for my sake will find it".(4)

Before we pursue this line of thought further there is a need to consider the positive elements of Christian fundamentalism and to attempt to understand at what point or points the fault lines occur.

A distressing lack of fellowship and welcome is so often the case for a person attending a mainstream church for the first time. The building may be a beautiful old Norman church, and packed full of a rich history of Christian worship. But the people may be stand-offish. The service may end with the minister uttering a mere pleasantry while shaking one's hand, and you leave the church without anyone else in the congregation having spoken to you. The experience in a fundamentalist church is rather different. There will be a warm welcome. People will evince interest in you as a newcomer.

The congregation will seem lively; there will be plenty of events going on. There will be an opportunity to join various groups for prayer, Bible study and so forth. And once one starts attending such a church regularly, there is a feeling of finding one's place in a seemingly secure set-up. There will soon also be involvement on the various church rotas and there will probably be also social events.

In short, one starts to become part of a *group* which has its own tightly defined parameters. And there is safety in being part of such a group which has its leaders, who have supposedly a vision for the church's future and who can be trusted to make all the important decisions. To be part of a warm group fellowship is in-itself a very positive thing. To feel needed by others and to feel on their 'wave-length' fosters at least some participating degree of sociality as opposed to, say a downright hedonistic, self-centred life-style. To be involved in worship which is animated and allows for a high degree of congregational participation, compared to a mechanical rendering of liturgical worship seems on a surface level to be both positive and democratic. Above all it is a good thing to be 'clear' about exactly what one believes as a Christian. And at least the fundamentalist can say in a nutshell what he or she believes rather than hum and ha about it. God, Christ and the Holy Spirit and their relevant doctrines are all taken seriously. The urgent sense of Christ's costly salvation and the need to alert men, women and children to it is a great positive which often shames the rather lethargic, latitudinarian attitude of many episcopal churches. It is of course totally in keeping with St. Paul and the early Christians to have a clear, burning and fervent attitude of commitment towards proclaiming Christ's gospel. It is absolutely right that there should be 'fundamentals' in Christian faith, just as there should be 'fundamentals' in other religious faiths. So too, should there be some 'fundamentals' in each of the various sciences and humanities. In fact it would be impossible to do any work at all in the sciences or humanities (or anything else such as business) without 'fundamentals', without at least some degree of acknowledgement of universals; in short, if there were no *a priori* accepted truths, facts or formulas there would be nothing to measure anything else against. For instance, what biologist today would completely reject the concept of evolution? Every biologist may have a slightly different view about evolution, but surely in the main there are few who would reject it outright. And even supposing some biologists do reject evolution as a conception, they would still have to find some alternative conception. Fundamentals of some sort are essential, for life's various modes all spring from some form or other of a base. You cannot build a house or any object without a base.

A base is thus a fundamental. Nothing can hold together or stay together without some form of given fundamentals. At least the Christian fundamentalist realises this. He or she realises in an urgent sense that all life springs from Christ who is in the Father; that our human base is predicated on the divine base. Without Christ we have nothing but our chicanery of sin with all its fantasies. For sin at root is fantasy, insubstantiality, precisely because it has no real base; the fundamental linkage with reality – with God the Father –

having been cut off by human hubris. And the latter along with all ego-inspired overreaching is naturally riddled with fantasy.

Thus far we can agree that generally the usual Christian fundamentalist – unless he or she is a complete fraud – is in receipt of a real 'religious experience'- whatever its degree of intensity. And this genuine experience has with it the beneficial effect of making the person in question aware of another more important dimension than that of the materialistic. Flowing from this revelatory discovery there is usually a second corollary, the awareness of personal sin, and thus the realization that all is not well in the state of the human soul. Thirdly, closely allied to this realization is the corresponding conviction that God in Christ is a loving and forgiving Father. Fourthly, there is usually a concern to share this religious experience with non-believers; a desire to proclaim that God exists, is Love, and his Son, Jesus Christ is a risen living Lord. The fifth important thing resulting from this religious experience is the inculcation of a reverence for God's Word, the holy scriptures. Here there is no cold scientific scepticism but rather both eagerness and respect. So these are the main positives which require some degree of awareness, personal change, love and humility in those who adhere to them. They are all 'fundamentals' which are vital to Christianity, and thus form an important basis for anyone seriously engaging on the Christian 'way'.

With all these key essentials in place, where then does the fault line of Christian fundamentalism occur? The whole problem, it seems to me, lies in the failure not to go beyond using the above mentioned basics in a merely defensive and de-creative way. The great fundamentals of the faith such as Creation, the Incarnation, the Cross, and the Resurrection, are used only as components of a kind of grand transcendental security system. This is where fundamentalism stops. And this is the problem, the fault line; that which is left out of the picture. Any form of extreme conservatism always involves the practice of omission. It is perhaps its sins of omission which constitute the worse aspects of Christian fundamentalism.

Let us now go back to the 'positive' picture previously outlined of the person who has found a welcoming and lively place of fundamentalist worship. But what happens next in terms of this person's spiritual pilgrimage? Once you are settled in a fundamentalist church (whether its actual denomination type is Pentecostal, Baptist, Methodist, Episcopal or whatever) you tend to go along with the group. You do not try to 'rock the boat' by pointing out that there are different approaches which can be made to the problems and issues of Christian faith. The church group you are in becomes a substitute for outside reality. It becomes a safe environment where one is cocooned from all that is unpleasant in the reality of world injustice, pain and suffering. The genuine religious experience instead of being an opening door to a new life of exciting, challenging and often arduous pilgrimage (as in the case of Christian from *Pilgrim's Progress*) becomes instead a point of fixation. There is no desire to go beyond this original experience; one becomes more and more jealously attached to it. But worse than this, God himself becomes limited to its confines! Perhaps here someone might point out that all who have had genuine experiences of God's transcendent 'otherness' have a right to jealously guard and remember them as being key religious moments. However, I am not disparaging such experiences but merely making the point that it is a serious mistake to attempt to use them as a kind of perpetual spiritual credit card, for in doing so any further Christian growth in maturity is undoubtedly seriously impaired or even forfeited. Clearly, in the case of John Wesley, his experience on 24th May, 1738 of feeling his heart "strangely warmed" (5) was a central moment never to be forgotten, but there is no indication in his long active Christian life that this particular moment was an arrival at a perfected spiritual state which required no further development. The significance of conversion or 'peak' experiences lies in the assurance that is given of Christ's presence rather than in the assurance of having successfully climbed some ladder of spiritual perfection.

Poverty, injustice and impending ecological disasters are all generally gaping great holes of omission for the fundamentalist who is happy and contented in his apparently secure church group setting. There is indeed grievous ignorance of the above mentioned issues, but is it merely just a straightforward matter of cognition deficiency? Rather, is it not more the case of self-imposed ignorance? Is it not based upon the deep-down fear of stepping out and attempting to understand why other people think as they do and why they thus hold the views that they do? The fundamentalist far from having no time *does not want to have time* for seeking to understand those who think differently from him or herself. Safety is seen in thinking along the same lines, and therefore anyone who comes into the group with new ideas (such as stirring up interest about third world injustices) is seen potentially as a threat by its self-styled leaders. Conformity is the name of the game. Anyone who attempts to breakaway from the numbing pattern of endlessly reciting basic Christian truths is seen as a wolf among the fold.

Human 'otherness' is a real fear for the fundamentalist. But this extends also to the conception of God! The element of divine mystery is therefore often lacking in fundamentalist churches. Why is this? For if God is Holy, as every devout fundamentalist would agree, why is the Creator made such an accommodating God who can be carried around easily and literally taken out of the pocket like a cheap little Bible tract? How can a God who is wholly 'other' even begin to be appreciated through the fundamentalists' crude diagrammatic tracts on how to be 'saved'? A God in the pocket is no God at all, let alone a God of infinite wonder, mystery and 'otherness'. The answer to these above questions seems to lie in the fundamentalist's demand for simple black and white contrasts; those who know the truth and those who don't; those who are specially Spirit-filled and those who are not; those who believe in the Bible as literal truth and those who do not; those who are 'saved' and those who are not.

Symbolism has always been a means of 'getting at' that which is beyond delineation by a factual approach. And therefore symbols are as old as humankind. Symbols denote that which is ungraspable; that which is immeasurable, and that which is unseen. As we have noted, the Christian fundamentalist's prime psychological drive is based upon a compelling need for security. Everything needs to be clear-cut in the fundamentalist's controlled environment, which is on one level a crude compensation for a world which is hopelessly out of joint. Symbolism therefore will not do. For one thing it suggests that things are *not* clear-cut; that in fact there is much more to human beings, life and the universe than that evinced by the average fundamentalist worship-goer. But also symbolism opens the door to many possibilities. The richness of a symbol (particularly of say, Christ's cross) is that it can encompass many facets of meanings which all lead to an enhancement of understanding the Christian faith. Again, this sense of many rich avenues of exploration runs against the grain of fundamentalism, which prefers to contain everything within a neat slide-rule. 'Exploration' is a dangerous word for a Christian fundamentalist; for the latter it suspiciously smacks of 'liberalism'. The hubris involved here seems to run thus: "We have arrived at the truth because we have experienced the Holy Spirit and this means God has shown us that everything in his Word is once and for all decided and crystal clear. Anyone who starts trying to explore new ways is trying to play around with what is fixed and therefore going astray". One could further say that the importance of Christian symbols is that they help keep, or better, signify the distance between the human and the numinous. In this respect they act as a kind of safeguard against human beings falling into the trap of treating God as if he was merely a very influential 'friend'. And surely this is a danger that the fundamentalist often (in most cases inadvertently) falls foul of. He or she seems to know God – Christ – all too well, and naively has no qualms in telling others what God does and doesn't like about certain human actions and beliefs; what God will most probably do or not do in the future, and so forth. In Short, God is created in the fundamentalist's own image, and the former can be counted upon to uphold the needs, opinions of the latter. So the fundamentalist is actually in control of God! The fundamentalist at this extreme level becomes little more than a puppet master who pulls the strings of a compliant manikin doll. And to espouse this type of false worship is to worship the golden calf of one's own ego, thereby tantamount to breaking the commandment not to make any graven image of God. The Creator is reduced to being little more than a convenient fiction who helps to bolster up the fears, prejudices and opinions of the fundamentalist. And this thus becomes a travesty of what should constitute the real Christian pilgrimage – the 'Way' of Christ. For instead of experiencing more fully the liberation of true freedom in Christ's forgiving love, the fundamentalist closes up both to God and the world (that is those who are not of his/her persuasion), becoming locked in a dogmatic, watertight compartment. This ultra fundamentalist will of course still claim loudly that he or she has absolute reverence for God, but ironically this reverence is merely reverence for their own jealously limited, little conception of God.

Religious symbolism in fact implies humility and reverence for it moves in the opposite direction to that of the literalist Biblical apprehension with which the fundamentalist produces his or her self-satisfying concrete certitude of faith. The symbol, by providing multiple windows in which to view its subject, is itself suggesting that the latter is worthy of far more consideration than just a simplistic black and white summation. While one would not wish to make an unkind, generalised denigration of historical Calvinism and its allied forms of Puritanism, it cannot but be noted that the contemptuous disregard for and often wanton physical destruction of church symbols was the start of a slippery slope down to the hollow, monochrome certitude of today's fundamentalist. Even the bareness of many of today's non-conformist churches and chapels (even though they may not house ultra-fundamentalists) attests to a tendency to have a restrictive and ultimately reductive approach to the Creator of the universe.

It could of course be claimed that the ultra-fundamentalist does indeed make use of some Christian symbols. For instance in the end-time scenarios so often evoked by those who belong to the so-called 'electronic church' of the United States there seems to be no amount of Biblical symbolism used. Thus, we have the apocalyptic image (taken from *Daniel, ch. 7)* of Christ seated on clouds, arriving in order to give out the final judgement upon the world. (The so-called 'rapture', based on the truly faithful people being immediately taken up to heaven when Christ comes again, is really a rather fanciful extrapolation from the relevant synoptic Biblical passages). Then there is the symbolism taken from *Revelation* which the electronic-fundamentalist church sees in gross literal terms as being a final cosmic combat between Christ and the Anti-

Christ. Accordingly, the fundamentalists with their strong Zionist attitude, see this last battle at Armageddon arising as the ultimate, victorious resolution of the current ongoing middle-east conflict. This battle will bring down the final curtain on human history; the righteous will drive out the unrighteous. Israel and the new Jerusalem will then be established for everlasting.

Because the ultra-fundamentalists are using these apocalyptic symbols in a gross literalist way, the latter are robbed of their proper richness of multi-functional meanings and mystery. As usual the fundamentalist is attempting to exploit the Bible in order to present a simplistic explanation which wraps up everything beyond a doubt. So the fundamentalist does indeed use the Christian symbols, but only to ironically de-symbolise them into a redundant literalism. And just as there seems little Biblical warrant for the sectarian idea of the 'rapture', there also seems little Biblical evidence in *Revelation* pertaining to what happens at Armageddon, and which specific nations are exactly involved in it. Symbolism, as we have stressed, does not by nature give itself away to easy clear-cut explanations, and it is the crass mistake of the ultra-fundamentalists that by always desiring to reduce everything down to a literal comprehension, they impoverish themselves by ignoring the multi-layered power of symbols.

The other important point which emerges from all this is that the fundamentalist eschews any personal responsibility for doing anything to improve the lot of his fellow men and women. Everything is going to end soon; it is all out of the

Christian's hands, his or her job is just to concentrate on being righteous and faithful. God will bring about the demise of history very soon; as a Christian it is just a matter of saving as many as can be saved. The world itself is rotten and therefore doomed; all one can do as a Christian is to get those who have "seen the light" on board the ark as quickly as possible. Any responsibility for working to make God's uniquely created world a better and more just place for human beings, animals and the environment simply does not come into the equation. If everything devolves down in the end to a great cosmic contest between Christ and the anti-Christ, the fundamentalist feels he or she has no pressing need to get involved in the crushing burdens of human injustice. The only important thing is to make sure you and your loved ones and friends are on the 'winning side'. The fundamentalist is thus free from worry about the ugly consequences arising from the mess of a fallen world, but he or she is in another sense enslaved to an unbendingly harsh, black and white judgemental end-time view. The present is of no consequence because if you are in the 'right team' there is going to a wonderful future for you. The fundamentalist's concept of liberty is thus bound up with the eschatological future. In terms of the present there is no real freedom, for where there is lacking a stewardship responsibility for the world and its inhabitants, there can only be a craven subservience to authoritarian structures. Eric Fromm, in *The Fear of Freedom,* has shown how conducive it is for people who cannot cope psychologically with the burden of socio-political freedom, to submit to being governed by authoritarian ruling elites. In this respect Christian fundamentalists are deficient in true Christian freedom which should impinge upon and affect all areas of human life. Furthermore, because of their disinterest in the machinations of the socio-political world, they render themselves unfit to assess, value and judge properly any complicated moral matters pertaining to that milieu of which they are a part. The fundamentalists either leave such matters to their political masters or vainly seek ready-made, paste-in answers from the Bible.

But the Bible of course is not a cornucopia of exact solutions which can be applied willy-nilly to the complex moral issues which abound today. In order to resolve or genuinely attempt to resolve such issues people are required either with specialist knowledge or who are at the very least prepared to expend sufficient time and thought on the problems involved. This is not tantamount to saying that the Bible is simply irrelevant where these issues are concerned. If one truly professes Christian faith the Bible cannot be other than massively relevant to all moral issues. But the point is in how one uses the scriptures. The Ten Commandments and Christ's new exhortation for us to love our neighbour obviously comprise the Christian's standard bedrock of morality. Every complex moral issue touches upon these foundational principles at some point or other, but it will not do to seek to solve such difficult and highly contentious issues as say, immigration and euthanasia, by forcing an answer out of a Biblical text. For it must be surely evident that we must judge things in their proper socio-political contexts and therefore you cannot make a cast-iron precedent out of an incident which happened several thousand years ago in an ancient culture and thereby apply it *literally* to a situation arising in the twenty-first century. Christianity is above all else a living religion (its founder is after all a risen Lord) and to survive with any credibility it must of necessity adopt a creative response to each progressive development in human history. And surely the signal characteristic of *grace* is that it represents all that is *not* legalistic, rigid and thus incapable of adapting to the changes which occur in the human situation (whether such changes are connected with new viewpoints in science, sociality, politics, aesthetics or whatever). For there is an elasticity in the reaching out of God's love; God's grace is not beholden to legalist restraints. In fact, though many of the churches – particularly the ultra-conservatist ones – often fall behind the new developments in human history (the end of the African slave trade, voting rights for women, etc), God the Creator is of course always in control and at the cutting edge of all historical movements to betterment of the human race. God in Christ is not absent but in everything. It is only Christians who fall behind and thus become absent from what really matters, particularly when they substitute the suppleness of God's overarching, forgiving love for a cut-and dried Manichaean based dogma of goodness and badness, reward and punishment.

It is not a question that Christians are to have some sort of grandly indulgent attitude to all the changes that occur in our rapidly changing western culture. Christians are required even more so than atheists and agnostics to take all moral issues seriously and to use all the means of grace at their disposal to find pathways of light through the moral mazes of our time. If scripture is used in the radical and enlightened spiritual manner in which Christ used it, the harsh, unconstructive type of solutions (which in fact are only miserable, temporary answers) will be avoided. If Christ had stuck to the vigorous application of Mosaic law, he would have sided with the Scribes and Pharisees who meant to stone the woman caught in adultery (6), as per the ruling set down in *Leviticus*:

> "If a man commits adultery with another man's wife
> – with the wife of his neighbour – both the adulterer
> and the adulteress must be put to death" (7).

But here is precisely where Christ's new covenant of transcending grace overleaps the sterility of the old covenant law's dead hand. When law is administered in an attitude of unenlightened fundamentalism, it is then in direct conflict with the radically releasing love of Jesus Christ.

Perhaps one of the core reasons for the hatred directed against Christ by the Jewish authorities was due to the former showing up the bankruptcy of pursuing religion by means of an unbending legalism. It is Christ who on one recorded occasion defends his disciples' right to pluck and eat some ears of corn on the Sabbath. (8). It is Christ who on countless occasions maintains the right to heal the sick and crippled on the Sabbath. (9) And it is Christ who creatively re-defines the laws through the transcendence of grace in its dimension of unconditional compassion. It is Christ who again on countless occasions defies the rigorously observed exclusion taboos of the law concerning leprosy, and reaches out a healing hand to those so afflicted (10).

It is Christ who eats at the same table with tax gatherers, prostitutes and other despised and marginalized members of society. In so doing he is going against the Mosaic rulebook which is enforced so relentlessly by such groups as the Scribes and Pharisees. Add all this together and it is not surprising that Christ was building up for himself a massive backlash of legalistic, fundamentalist indignation and hatred. And ultimately it was this cumulative backlash of narrow-minded bigotry which helped, among other things, to put the Son of God on his cruel and shameful cross at Calvary.

We may remember a parabolic saying of Christ, recounted in the synoptic gospels:

> "...no one pours new wine into old wineskins. If he does, the wine will burst the skins, and both the wine and the wineskins will be ruined. No, he pours new wine into new wineskins" (11).

Jesus was probably referring to the old legalistically framed, Mosaic covenant which was no longer suitable for being the vehicle to hold the new abundant 'Kingdom' life contained in the 'living' covenant of his own divine, unconditional love. So the new wine is the new 'way' of Christ; his new way of looking at the deeper aspects of the human situation. It is the way of the 'Kingdom' not of the Scribal rulebook. It is "new wine" because it is no longer an endless minutia of rules which incur inexorable punishments or corresponding rewards; instead, it offers the graciousness of a forgiving God, capable of seeing into the innermost depths of the human heart and knowing all the mitigating factors involved in the tragic failure of human sin. The vision of God is enhanced through the advent of Jesus Christ. Thus the God of the "old wineskins", Jehovah, the wrathful, jealous God (even though he had always displayed mercy) is significantly modified to the extent of being endowed with the overriding characteristic of unconditional Fatherly love. After Jesus Christ no 'authentic' lover of God could purvey again the mistaken notion that God was some kind of oriental despot who made all his judgements according to unbending laws, and who had no interest in all the mitigating factors involved in the breaking of these laws.

Such a conception of God – and one has to accept that the *Old Testament* idea of God was based upon a series of very incomplete revelations – tended to portray a Creator who had little or even zero tolerance of sin. However, God as revealed by Jesus Christ, is in fact concerned with every facet of human life. It is not that Christ reveals a new better God as opposed to a supposedly earlier Creator, as in accordance with the second century Marcion heresy; on the contrary, Jesus reveals an expanded, fuller revelation of the *Old Testament* God; namely, a cosmic Father, replete with sympathetic understanding and compassion for the falleness and ensuing follies of the special 'beings' created in his own likeness. God had not changed, but with the Incarnation of Christ, there was now a glorious opportunity to witness within history the supreme example of how the Creator, himself, would cope with the practical, existential problems involved in being human. And despite the fact that the fundamentalists talk so much about the Father's saving love, they tend to give the impression that they have not really thought though properly the ramifications of Christ's new revelation of God. Even though apparently accepting Christ's New Covenant, they tend to cling to the older, more simplistic *Old Testament* ideas of a mighty despot who hates all who reject him and who will send all disbelievers to everlasting punishment. But this is not the God as revealed by Jesus Christ; not the God who is prepared to stop at nothing to find the 'lost sheep'; not the God who was prepared to accept his own rejection; not the God who was prepared to take upon himself the burden of human sin with all its overwhelming guilt. One cannot help but feel that the God of the fundamentalists is still bound up with the Old Covenant; that there is no real appreciation of the radically new 'way' of Christ, where forgiveness and its corollary of freedom issue not from the rigid rulebook, but rather out of an open-ended, deeply understanding and bottomless love. Jesus Christ, above all others, knew and knows how complicated and contradictory are the various facets which go up to make the human psyche. And that should be so not just experientially through the Incarnation experience, but also because Christ is the Creating Word who formed all things in the beginning:

> "Through him all things were made; without him nothing was made that has been made". (12)

In any intelligent debate or discourse on a particular concept, subject, situation, or whatever, it is highly likely that someone will at some point use phrases similar to: "..concerning this aspect of the problem..." or "there are certain aspects of this which I am not happy about"... and etc. When such a word as "aspect" or "aspects" is used it is usually because one wants to denote more specifically a particular area of a topic under discussion. One of the main characteristics of the centuries prior to the mid-twentieth century is the amount of generalisations used by historians, social commentators, artists, critics and other branches of academics. Generalisations can be useful as compact overviews of certain topics or situations but there is the obvious danger that something which has many facets (history is an obvious example) can be too simplified and as a result, even trivialised. If one now peruses, for instance, British history schoolbooks up to say, the mid-twentieth century, it cannot but be noted that everything reads too simplistically. Of course where the narrative portrays British foreign history, the assumption is naively of a benevolent, righteous colonial power dealing at times with noble warrior enemies, albeit, inferior human beings. History in this still largely unself-critical age, tends to be formulated on neat black and white contrasts. The notion of isolating the different factors – aspects – of a given topic or situation and subjecting some or each of them to a rigorous analysis, has still not properly arrived. A simplistic approach to something which is potentially very complicated must inevitably result in a more or less dangerous degree of falsification. Therefore, isolating the various elements of a topic and then focusing specifically on one or more of these elements is what is needed, although necessarily this is a far more exacting task. Due to Freud's pioneering and revelatory opening up of the unconscious dimension to human psychology and also due to various post-modern critiques, many of the old historical, sociological certainties have either become suspect or fallen under radical revision. In such an iconoclastic milieu as our contemporary period, many age-old certainties or traditions on the human level have disappeared or are in the process of disappearing. Consequently, it is thus now the general consensus that all serious discourse, discussion and commentary must be able to avoid simplistic generalisations and that the order of the day is discernment and the ability to scrutinize the different factors or facets which constitute the subject or situation in question.

The glass prism, with its many-sided reflecting areas, acts as a good symbol for denoting life's rich complexity. As each reflecting surface of the prism is a part of the whole, the act of isolating one particular surface and analysing it will bear fruit in terms of elucidating the prism as a totality. And this basic principle can be evidenced in all academic disciplines and thinking of any depth. Thus, for instance, a literary critic may write a book focusing on the aspect of military symbolism in say, the work of Edmund Spenser. This may at first seem reductive in its apparently limited scope, but it might very well be the case, that if properly handled by the critic, the studying of this particular aspect will result in a harvest of enhanced understanding and appreciation of Spenser's genius. For genius, just like history and any other serious topic, is multi-layered. It is the recognition that we can only fully appreciate the things of this world if we abandon the undiscriminating, pre-modern attitude of either-or. For it is only by isolating out the various factors involved in a situation or cultural construction that we can meaningfully and therefore, properly engage with it. To simplify a thing is often merely to lose it.

Simplistic analysis when dealing with something complex is reductionism, resulting in a seriously defective relationship with the subject, situation or concept in question.

And here we arrive at a salient point. The Christian fundamentalist, far from firmly grasping the essence of his or her faith, on the contrary, through a crassly mistaken reductionism, ironically achieves only a very weak grasp. The fundamentalist desires above all an absolute iron certainty in the matter of faith. And it is precisely this desire which stifles his or her growth to maturity in the faith. In St. John's gospel, the disciple Philip, still unconvinced by Jesus' assertion that he who has seen him has seen the Father, exclaims, perhaps rather petulantly:

> "Lord, show us the Father and that will be enough for us". (13)

Philip is demanding what every Christian fundamentalist demands: literalism. Christ's subsequent response evinces some degree of exasperation at Philip's failure. But it is the later, risen Christ's recorded answer to Thomas' doubt which gives us the most emphatic indication of what the true meaning of faith is:

> "...Because you have seen me, you have believed; blessed are those who have not seen and yet have believed". (14)

Real Christianity involves the radicalism of going beyond

literalism. Faith is itself a symbol of trust in the unseen, of stepping out into the darkness. There is indeed some form of a Kierkegaardian leap involved in a living faith (maybe only a graduated series of little leaps), for there is risk in an authentic following of the 'way' of Christ. Faith is not certainty. As Miguel de Unamuno has well said:

"A faith that does not doubt is a dead faith" (15).

And after all, even Thomas' doubting of the risen Christ paradoxically resulted in his great affirmation of faith: "My Lord and my God!" (16).

The Christian fundamentalists consider themselves radical, but this is only by ironically narrowing the definition of radicalism. For them, holding onto the literal truth and not allowing any slightest deviations from that mode of apprehension is what constitutes being a radical Christian. They see themselves as upholding the kernel of Christianity while many others seem bent on relentlessly eroding its foundations. They see themselves as radical because they feel they are not diluting the gospel; that they are telling people the straight Biblical truth. Their religious world does not allow for any uncertainties and modifications of viewpoints. But this is not the radical gospel of Jesus Christ. It is not the gospel of personal risk, whereby one associates with despised sinners such as tax-collectors and harlots, thus causing affront to the water-tight morality of the religious authorities. Radicalism, by definition aims at bringing in a new way of going about things. It is clear that this greatly characterises Christ's earthly ministry. Fundamentalism's only concern is to make everyone else conform to its own likeness. When St. Paul gave his famous injunction in *Romans:*

> "Do not conform any longer to the pattern of this world, but be transformed by the renewing of your mind" (17)

he was not enjoining Christians to become fundamentalists, but rather enjoining them to be the exact opposite. Namely, to be people who strove to weave into their lives the rich living tapestry of Jesus Christ, who took each human being he encountered as an unique God-created individual. Christ's only law for dealing with proud and broken humanity was the law of Grace. Hence there were no pre-conceived barriers towards anyone, no matter what their race or situation, or what they had become through sin:

> "I am the bread of life. He who comes to me will never go hungry, and he who believes in me will never be thirsty...and whoever comes to me I will never drive away" (18).

The only true and legitimate power is the sacramental power of God's Holy Spirit, for it is a power which ministers the unconditional love of God in Christ. Like the father in the parable of the Prodigal Son, there are no judgemental questions asked and instead only a display of joy that one who was lost has returned. Similarly, the shepherd in the parable of the lost sheep, does not berate the animal for getting lost, but instead carries it home over his shoulders with joyfulness. Here is the only proper usage of power – spiritual power – which forgives and saves the world rather than condemns it. Fundamentalism does not offer the unconditional forgiveness of Jesus Christ; rather, it offers salvation only as a *conditional* reward for conformity to a new code of legalism made up of set-attitudes and conventions of worship behaviour. Certainly, the Creator cannot pour out all the blessings he wishes to on recalcitrant, unregenerate individuals, but can it really be the case that the God as revealed by Christ is *unable* to love people until they profess faith in him? Fundamentalists effect a disastrous disservice to Christian witness when they thus (presumably unwittingly) portray God as a kind of tyrant who is only prepared to love people when they obey him. Yet on this point scripture could not be clearer:

> "...God demonstrates his own love for us in this: While we were still sinners, Christ died for us".(19)

> "This is love: not that we loved God, but that he loved us and sent his Son as an atoning sacrifice for our sins".(20)

CHAPTER 2

CHRISTIAN LIBERAL CONFORMISM

Recorded in St. John's gospel is the famous or perhaps infamous encounter between Jesus Christ and Pontius Pilate, the procurator of Judaea. Towards the end of that encounter there is a classic moment of significance between the accused and interrogator:

> "You are a king, then!" said Pilate. Jesus answered, "You are right in saying I am a king. In fact, for this reason I was born, and for this I came into the world, to testify to the truth. Everyone on the side of truth listens to me". "What is truth?" Pilate asked. (1)

Here is perhaps the first example of the extreme liberalist mentality in the face of Christianity – in fact in the face of its founder, Jesus Christ. "What is truth?" is the arch-liberal question. It is true that the flustered Pilate did not stay to pursue with Jesus any possible answers to this question, but then for the over-developed liberalist mentality there are no final, absolute answers to a question such as "truth". The whole mentality of 'liberalism' is unconcerned with transcendental absolutes, rather its concern is with what is horizontal, with what is measurable and contingent in human sociological terms. Thus, Pilate's throw-away remark seems very modernistic; perhaps the type of laconic question Nietzsche or Freud would have thrown back at one of their conventional contemporaries who was bandying with the word "truth". It seems to me that this short but classic encounter between Christ and Pilate forms a very good starting point for what I wish to say about the way that western liberal Protestantism becomes a stumbling block (in my opinion) to the authentic Christian gospel. For, as we note in the above quoted passage of St. John, Jesus' double assertion that his "mission" is to "testify to the truth" and that "Everyone on the side of truth" will ally themselves with him. These are indeed staggering statements to come from a man of flesh and blood. If a person in our post-modern society made such gigantic assertions they would be roundly condemned as a fundamentalist fanatic. The choice, then, is starkly clear: either Jesus Christ was a badly deluded fanatic or he was, as the incarnate Son of God, a uniquely sinless and morally perfect human being, justly entitled to make such staggering claims for himself.

Despite the obvious mental and physical strain he was under, Jesus evinces a remarkable self-control and assurance which is in stark contrast to the increasingly worried Pilate. But these deliberate and measured words of Christ are the outcome of no mere fanatical bravado. Christ has already been insulted, humiliated, beaten and is in the final stages of a cooked-up trial for his life. He already knows what the personal cost will involve: the utter public disgrace and vile physical torture of crucifixion. Christ was never some sort of public sophist or theological boaster but it is in this final encounter with those in corrupt human authority that the Saviour must now assert publicly his Messiahship. It is now that he must make public what he had previously said only for the benefit of his band of followers:

> "I am the way and the truth and the life. No-one comes to the Father except through me". (2)

Here we also collide with the post-modern liberalist view that there can be such a thing as an ultimate objective 'truth'. (Objective truth in liberalism is confined to contingent truth in all its various scientific, economic and socio-historical categories; it is the result of cold analysis and dissection). However, Christ's ultimate, objective 'truth' is a living 'truth', incarnate in the human flesh and blood of a Jewish born man who has suffered great abuse, gross injustice and who now faces an ignominious and hideous death. Both the Jewish and Roman authorities rejected the claim of Christ that he is in himself "the way and the truth and the life".

The Jewish authorities reject Christ from their own fundamentalist standpoint which is not wide enough to grasp the liberating love of God which overleaps the minutia of the strictly interpreted Mosaic law. The Roman authority under

Pilate rejects Christ because its so-called religious tolerance does not extend to accepting any ultimate homage beyond that of Caesar. Either way entails the rejection of Christ as absolute living truth. And today's ultra-liberal Christian similarly rejects Christ, in that the former will not tolerate a claim which smacks to their mind of both arrogant exclusiveness and out-of-date transcendentalism. Once again the nails of rejection are driven into Christ; he is crucified by political correctness which will not tolerate that anyone should dare to claim they are the divine Son of God. And this rejection to varying extents characterises not only the ultra-liberalists but filters through to even many mainstream liberal Christians. My only answer to the charge of Christ's claim being one of arrogant exclusiveness is to say that the Judaic-Christian God as Creator of the universe cannot be anything else than 'other' to human creation. But of course if you reduce God to a 'ground of being', you de-size God to merely a convenient abstract phrase which incurs no political incorrectness. Moreover, a 'ground of being' is hardly equivalent to Christ's living Way, his Truth. In the words of Miguel de Unamuno: "Ideas do not live or love"(3). Paul Tillich's favoured phrase: "ground of being", can too easily be used as a convenient way of excluding Jesus Christ from any theological discussion. I would suggest that using such a phrase may well be seen as a safe means of talking about Christianity without supposedly offending anybody, and one of the things many liberal protestants are concerned about is straying into the area of political un-correctness. Naturally, the whole *raison d'etre* of "political correctness" is about staying within the safe boundaries of a scheme of *laissez-faire* conformist ideas. Any remarks critical or evaluative of such a set-up are deemed to be elitist.

One can immediately see that in the above respect *liberalism* is as touchy as *fundamentalism* with regard to any serious criticism aimed at its current ideological premises. But the problem involved with assessing *liberalism* is nevertheless far more complicated than assessing *fundamentalism,* for the latter tends to be more easy to assess because of its inherent limitations which preclude the production of any highly concentrated thought. However, there are many strands and many varying degrees to liberalism. There is by no means any real consensus grouping and so as a movement it is somewhat fragmented and untidy compared to fundamentalism. The problem, then, of trying to give some sort of compact overview of contemporary Christian liberalism is due to its sheer range of differing and sometimes contradictory approaches. It does not parallel the type of consistency and coherency of views which one can generally posit of fundamentalism. Nevertheless, I believe there are certain basic characteristics which run through – or form the bedrock – of most current Christian liberalism. What I aim to do here is to map out these general contours and then to look at how, if taken to extremes, these can lead not to radical Christianity but rather to a sheltered conformism disguised by so-called "radical" new ways of theological thinking.

In my introduction I suggested that human autonomy could be suitable as a basic starting point definition of liberalism. Of course what I mean here is not an open mandate for human anarchy but rather, subject to necessary social checks and balances (which foster the safety of fellow citizens), an assumption that human freedom is intrinsic to human life. And I believe virtually all liberals would agree with this. Thus liberalism has this basic emphasis on the autonomy of the individual; that a person has the right to live not as a slave or serf, and also has a right to freedom of conscience in terms of being able to disagree non-violently with the way things are run politically and socially along with being able to pursue their own chosen sets of beliefs. But precisely because of this view protestant liberalism tends to react against the notion of absolute truth. There is in the modern and post-modern liberal consciousness the underlying assumption that human freedom and universals are simply not compatible. Freedom is thus posited on the relativity and contingency of life; there can be no longer any grand answering patterns to the riddle of the universe. On this relativistic view, science chiefly, but also to a much lesser extent the humanities will gradually clear up most of the technical problems of human knowledge. The underlying assumption being that this entails a continual process of tackling each bit of contingency and then relating it to other bits so that progress will be steadily made. The various answers are thus relative to their contingent context. And indeed, the very process of methodically digging for step-by-step answers would itself demonstrably enshrine for the liberalist the whole rationalist basis of human autonomy.

What of course undergirds this belief in human autonomy – the right to pursue one's own pathway whether it is in just basic day-to-day living or in scientific investigation or in the various arts – is the notion of *tolerance*. Therefore the freedom to be an autonomous agent is predicated on the right to be free from anything which can be classed as oppressive. Connected with this is an assumption that it is right to hold a sceptical attitude towards anything which claims to be above or beyond this neo-Darwinian world of contingency. For anything that is beyond or can bypass the latter would have to involve some sort of universals and absolutes. And the fear of liberal Protestantism (particularly in its ultra forms), is of an overarching ultimate pattern interfering and indeed spoiling the increasingly specialised and self-sufficient independence of post-modern man and woman.

Self-sufficiency is very much a key aspect of the liberal Protestant psychology. And one can see how it naturally arises from liberalism's fundamental and allied beliefs in the right of toleration, the right to be sceptical and the right to human freedom. Now none of these rights are in question, *per se*, but what is of concern is that in my view they have led away from the real gospel of Christ and instead resulted in a neo-Feuerbachian Christianity, which is to say not a Christianity at all but rather a self-conceited infatuation with humankind's own abilities and achievements. In short, the horizontal is everything.

However, before going further, it is important to do justice and attempt to make a full acknowledgement of the significant positives of protestant liberalism. We can, for convenience class these under two umbrella headings: *Toleration* and *Adequate knowledge*. Firstly, *toleration* is obviously vital for any degree of Christian unity, as long as it is toleration which has a genuine desire for understanding the other party rather than just being nothing but a lax accepting attitude. Allied to a genuine tolerance is openness to other denominations and different faiths. This can only be a great benefit for healing political and cultural misunderstanding, but of course there needs to be awareness that whether it be denominations or different religions, there will still be certain unbridgeable areas. Thus to take some obvious examples, the Roman Catholic mass, the veneration of the Pope will always be stumbling blocks for most Protestant denominations, and liturgy will always be a stumbling block for such denominations as say, Baptists and Pentecostals. But certainly, anything which strives to bring people together, casting away the fear and distrust engendered in racial and cultural differences can only be doing the work of Christ.

The history of the institutionalised Christian Church from Constantine onwards has only been too riddled with and pockmarked by intolerance. How many so-called saints such as for example, Cyril of Alexandria and St. Augustine have displayed lack of charity and even downright, malicious Machiavellian power-play against those who held differing views of the faith! The absolutism and vehemence with which many of the great church fathers and leading lights of the medieval age attacked any slight deviations of Christian thought seems aeons away from the Messiah who befriended those who had deviated greatly from the commandments of the God of Israel. Even when we come to the Reformation tolerance does not greatly improve. We can only ask why Luther could so often display such an intolerant and unforgiving attitude to those who had, in his view, fallen foul of sin. One only has to read his catechisms and follow his disputes with Zwingli and Erasmus to wonder at Luther's absolutist and irascible attitude. And could not Calvin have done the charitable thing that Christ would have done with regard to the doctrinal trouble-maker, Servetus? Could Calvin not have spared the executioners hand on a man who despite his mistakenness and overreaching presumption was not inherently evil? Again, to take a further example, even when one examines the documented views of the erudite, principled martyr, Sir Thomas More, one finds an astonishing amount of the worse kind of opinionated intolerance directed against those who favoured the reformation cause. More evinces a tone of self-righteous satisfaction when mentioning the untimely deaths of martyred reformers (4), many of whom, such as the talented and likeable young theologian, John Frith, he relentlessly persecuted. Thus, one could go on in citing examples where an inbuilt Christian institutional culture has infected even its greatest human products with intolerance. It is enough then to even briefly remember how destructive and brutal lack of tolerance can be and how it irresponsibly throws away the olive branch of reconciliation, tearing down rather than building up Christ's Kingdom work. It is clear then, that we can be grateful to liberalism for re-emphasising the non-rejectional approach of Christ to *all* who came across his pathway:

"...whoever comes to me I will never drive away" (5).

And one can also reflect on the fact that *Acts* (ch.17, 16-34) records how St. Paul, on Mars Hill, was quite prepared to debate Christianity with the philosophers of Athens. Indeed,

St. Paul followed his Master's liberal trait of non-rejectionism, and was always prepared to debate his faith at synagogues despite all hostility and risk to his own person. St. Paul is often wrongly considered to be an arch kind of intolerant fundamentalist, yet it is he who is recorded as saying:

> "I have become all things to all men so that by all possible means I might save some"(6)

What is becoming "all things to all men" but not the operation of a tolerating, Christ-like understanding? How could an intolerant person possibly declare that he or she is prepared to creatively get inside the place where the other person is "coming from"? Intolerance is in a rush; it is in too much of a hurry to spend time seeing where the other person is "coming from". If St. Paul had been the intolerant person his many detractors claim him to have been, the authentic gospel of Christ's saving and forgiving love would never have spread as it did do. Thus a basic tolerance is fundamental to the spreading and fruitfulness of God's grace.

Toleration of course in its positive rather than mere lazy aspect implies a willingness to achieve a better and thus enhanced understanding of the other person. And this can only be done through a more patient rather than judgemental attitude toward the 'other'. Christ's warnings about falling into the judgemental mode are crystal clear:

> "Do not judge, or you too will be judged. For in the same way you judge others, you will be judged..." (7)

The liberalist, unlike the fundamentalist, will be more likely to understand that negatively judging another person necessarily involves feelings of superiority and thus inculcates self-righteousness. This of course is not the way of Christ, for judging others automatically involves the erecting of barriers; those who do the judging imply that they have a higher basis of religious morality. But anyone who reads, for instance, Bunyan's: *Grace Abounding*, will realize that the struggle for personal holiness is not necessarily crowned by being able to finally live on a higher spiritual plateau. Rather, the Christian, like Bunyan will find their pilgrimage somewhat like a game of snakes and ladders. Sin is certainly a human constant in the theological thought of Sir Thomas More, and for him duality is inescapable, with a person "now up now downe, now fallynge by synne and now rysynge agayne by grace" (8). Life is a topsy-turvy affair and being a Christian does not magically render one immune from our in-built flaws of fallen nature and all the stresses and strains connected with the varieties of human contacts and relationships.

The Christian liberal will thus be nearer to Christ's attitude than the fundamentalist in respect to having more of a disposition to treat 'others' in an equalitarian sense. The vulgar sense of "being spiritually in the know" will at least not be so blatant (it may of course operate at a more subtle level) as it sadly so often is amongst many fundamentalists. The latter tend to take a dim view of those who are supposedly outside the Kingdom of Heaven. Again, the fundamentalists are guilty of stipulating rules and regulations for the entry into the Kingdom. But Jesus' parables concerning the Kingdom tend to confirm a largess and benevolence which tallies far more with liberalism than fundamentalism. Consider, for instance the image of the net:

> "...the kingdom of heaven is like a net that was let down into the lake and caught all kinds of fish. When it was full, the fishermen pulled it up on the shore".(9)

This could actually mean in one sense that God does not leave any single human being alone but catches them all up to some degree or other in his Kingdom of Love. The important truth here is that no person can said to be left in a God-less state. God and his Son through the Holy Spirit are not absent, but rather bound up in everything. However, the fundamentalists would categorically argue that unless you specifically confess faith and join a particular church you are not saved – not part of God's Kingdom. But the net parable would suggest that God is very near to all his human creation, and catches them up in his love whether they accept or reject him. The intelligent liberal Christian will realize that although the proclamation of the gospel is important it is by grace rather than by human persuasion or coercion that people are "netted" into the Kingdom. There is therefore the sense that we are all "accidentally" in God's net, and that if only we knew it we could jubilantly accept this glorious benefit as did the merchant in the parable of the priceless pearl (10). The liberal Christian then, will be more likely to accept that faith is not a prerogative of merely a more " holy person" but rather that it is the result of acceptance of the fact that God is *already* bound up and working in all humanity. God is for *all* people. He operates from a level playing field; there are no pre-ordained elect. All have an invitation to the Kingdom and through Christ's redeeming work are all as it were within entrance of the new spiritual dimension of "resurrection life". God's love is equal to every human being, man, woman and child. Family and other wider social situations may stack the cards against some unfortunate human beings, but God's love will always consistently deal out a fair hand.

Secondly, for liberal Protestantism there is the importance of having *adequate knowledge*. Thus, for instance, the emphasis laid upon understanding the modern and post-modern world is very beneficial, if not vital, to the faith. It is obvious that one must as much as possible try to understand the mechanisms which undergird and drive our modern world. One must appreciate the important advances in science where they further our knowledge of not only our own bodily mechanisms but also of the workings and principles (such as evolution) which apply to our whole planet. Yet even in the twenty-first century it is to be deeply lamented that certain States in America, because of their blinkered theology of "Creationism", will not allow evolution to be taught in schools. This withholding of such a foundational deposit of knowledge and understanding borders on a neo-inquisitional kind of intolerance. The renowned American theologian, Reinhold Niebuhr, while recognising evolution does seem to threaten the sense of human uniqueness, nevertheless says categorically:

"There can be no question about the futility of the

effort to guard the idea of the uniqueness of the human person by resisting and defying the evidence of the biological scientists in regard to the evolution of natural forms. This is the more true since it is an accepted fact and truth that man is related to the natural order and is in a sense an animal".(11)

History continually attests to the fact that with a greater increase in knowledge human beings of necessity have to re-adjust their way of perceiving the world and themselves. This can of course be a very stiff challenge, yet nevertheless human life is in many different ways a continuous challenge. We do not live in paradise! Life in a "fallen" world is in many ways both a burden and an ongoing struggle. But blindly clinging to convenient and simplistic ideas does not help matters and the fundamentalist Christian only appears as an anarchism when he or she doggedly re-iterates outdated modes of theological literalism, such as simplistic ideas of reward and punishment. To cling to such outdated modes requires a constant refusal to give any serious consideration to the various issues which form the core of today's modernity. Rather than merely to shout louder the simplistic fundamentalist mantras, what is in fact needed is a creative Christian approach to the modern situation. This means at least some form of engagement rather than just a constant, blanket denial. Christian liberalism, to its credit, appreciates in theory at least the need for a Christianity which is alive and relevant to its contemporary milieu. Whether of course such liberalism does build up a truly creative approach or merely a *laissez-faire* relativistic approach is of course another matter.

It can hardly be overstated how essential is it is for a person to acquire adequate knowledge in any subject field which they intend to absorb their interest in. Naturally, it is just as important for a Christian to have as much knowledge about his or her faith as possible as it is for a scientist to have as much relevant knowledge as possible appertaining to his or her relevant field of work. Of course "adequate knowledge" can either be construed as having just a little more than a rock-bottom basic understanding or possessing a far greater competence of comprehension. With regard to understanding the holy scriptures we must acknowledge the great benefits ushered in as a result of new methods of historical, contextual criticism. Advances in more accurate biblical translation from the Greek and Hebrew sources received powerful impetuses as a result of both the Renaissance and the Reformation. (We have only to think of the groundbreaking work of a translator such as for instance, Erasmus, who harboured within his wide-ranging cosmopolitan genius many enlightened traits which could be aligned with the modern liberalist mentality). The nineteenth century heralded the rise of the historical critical method which has in its various modifications of approach continued to be a major factor in most contemporary theological schools of learning. The desire to study in a more methodical and scrutinizing way is clearly a central plank of the ongoing legacy of classical Protestant liberalism. Moreover, it seems eminently reasonable to suggest that a Christian ought to be aware in some degree of the socio-historical contexts of scripture and its processes of transmission, as well as possess a basic awareness of the merits and limitations of various bible translations. At its best the principle of a more vigorous critical appraisal of the truths of scripture, as evinced by many great biblical scholars and preachers through the past hundred years or so, has enhanced and enriched the faith of many members of the laity. And this can only be a good thing for the Kingdom of Christ. Protestantism from Lutheranism onwards, with its emphasis on adequate scriptural knowledge, has certainly never lacked concern for the dissemination of Christianity by the mode of teaching. Although Lutheranism itself under Luther never approached any real modern kind of liberalism, nevertheless it helped to open up channels for a far more directly biblical, expositional teaching compared to the rigid scholastic dogmatics of much of the previous medieval and Renaissance ages. And even today when one re-reads the sermons of Anglican-Calvinistic puritan preachers of say, the 17th century, one is struck by the in-depth biblical knowledge on display; such a confident grasp of scripture and the ability to transmit it would before the advent of the Lutheran revolution, a century earlier, indeed have been a rarity in the clergy.

But what now of the minuses of Christian liberalism? Paradoxically the weaknesses of the latter flow out of its very strengths. It is abundantly clear that liberalism, by tending to look at the *relative merits* of a person or a situation, does well to eschew the sort of blind absolutism of the fundamentalist. But taking this relativistic approach to its logical extreme inevitably leads to a denial of any sort of absolute truth. For if life merely revolves around contingency and relativity, anyone adopting the notion of absolute truth will tend to be viewed as regressing into intolerance. Yet the gospels are shot through and through with "absolutism", from the harsh forceful words of John the Baptist onwards to the miracles of Christ, and the latter's various recorded statements (particularly the famous "I am" sayings found in St. John's gospel). And all this culminating and being capped with Christ's once and for all redeeming death on the Cross, his resurrection and ascension. Many liberalist (and not all are necessarily extremists) deeply question or outrightly deny all or most of the above "absolutisms". Christ is then reduced to the historical Jesus of Nazareth; Jesus the good man, the healer, the moral educator, the heroic man, the great prophet, but not the very own, precious Son of the Creator God.

Christ, despite being bestowed with all the above great accolades is made *relative*. He merely represents and spotlights all the best qualities of civilized *homosapiens*. And if Christ is merely the best on a purely earthly level then he is just a Feuerbachian mirror of human goodness at its optimum functioning capability. If this is the case we only have to admire Christ and strive to use him as a kind of creative self-help, guide-to-living book. The problem can thus be seen that liberalism easily veers into Unitarianism. And when this happens we are left with a kind of modern humanistic version of "adoptionism". A non-divine Christ, who is not the crucified, risen and glorified Son, sitting at the right-hand of the Father, but rather a great humanitarian who has been "adopted" from below rather than above as an ethical role model for the good of civilization. On another level there is also operative in liberalism a subtle re-working of Docetism. And here even the historical solidity of Christ is abrogated in favour of symbols and abstractions such as the already mentioned: "ground of being". Many ultra-liberalists in this modern version of Docetism tend to view Christ as only a guiding spiritual symbol. Jesus becomes a lighted candle but never the fully engaged human Christ who lived in Palestine, meeting the needs of all who came across his pathway.

Toleration itself is double-edged. As we have already seen, in its positive aspect of respecting other people rather than condemning them, it is very close to the Christian ethic of serving and loving others. Yet the Christian ethic of service and love is not based on relativity; it is an absolute ethic, for one either chooses to fully accept or reject the grace of God which is held out by the outstretched arms of the "suffering servant". But ever since the enlightenment, toleration has in effect implied an increasing uncertainty with regard to the notion of ultimate truth. However, the underbelly of toleration has always been scepticism. One can be like a Roman stoic philosopher and accept the cruel absurdity of the universe; one can by determined acts of will-power tolerate everything, even in the end the idea of a painful death. But this is merely a toleration laced with a concealed, despairing scepticism, for no one in the depths of their hearts can really pretend to a *total and disinterested toleration*. Toleration in its *laissez-faire* aspect merely degenerates into conformity. One accepts the other person in an outward, superficial egalitarian sense, while reserving the right to observe them from a hermetically sealed world of superiority. Here, in this negative form of toleration, there can be no proper meeting point with the other person. To return again to the meeting between Pilate and Christ – the former was quite prepared to be tolerant and give the latter his freedom, but this was merely a negative tolerance; Pilate had no interest in pondering with any depth on who Jesus really was. Thus the Roman governor's cynical tolerance acted as a barrier to the grace of God, which confronted him in the person of Jesus Christ. By contrast, Christ, truly fulfilling Isaiah's great prophecies of the "suffering servant", displayed the real virtues of positive toleration. The Saviour while standing resolutely for his own divine position of absolute truth, did not however deride his oppressor. Christ stood firm but as the "suffering servant" he tolerated the right of his opponent to have the earthly power to dispose of himself even unto death by crucifixion.

There is also another way in which we can consider toleration as double-edged. Intolerance tends to be usually viewed as the *intolerance of others*, and this can be a very convenient projection, for the concept of sin and thus personal guilt, has been largely forgotten or ignored by liberal Protestantism. It is clear that liberalism finds the very word "sin" rather unpalatable, stirring up perhaps medieval ideas of guilt, punishment and the stewing pot flames of Hell; hence liberalism's erasing of the word "sin" and its replacement by the word "intolerance". Of course there is among the existentialists (such as Sartre) and other thinkers the notion of *personal responsibility*, but on the whole, the general liberal view is that what is wrong is down to the intolerance of those who hold extreme or even fanatical religious, political or racial beliefs and opinions. There is thus in liberalism criminality instead of sinfulness. The condition of sin does not exist, but what does exist are criminal acts of evil, prisons and the corresponding counselling therapies and mental hospitals which aim to diagnose the causes and attempt to effect some degree of remedy. However, the human condition with all its impenetrable perversity continues unabated. It was precisely because the great 19th century Russian novelist, Dostoevsky, knew how deep evil ran in the human psyche that he railed so effectively in his writings against the naive idealism of socialist engineering. (12). Sigmund Freud's land-mark discovery of the unconsciousness and its dominating significance in terms of the human condition, merely collaborates Dostoevsky's view, that to a large extent people are not fully in control of themselves but rather governed by dark irrational impulses and forces. And here we are in a curious way back to evil in its sense of *personal sin*.

Dostoevsky was a believer in the Christian faith and Freud was not, yet both of them come to the same conclusion that there is a fundamental disorder – even chaos – within the unknown depths of the human psyche. It is not the top, outward layer which is important, it is rather the unseen layers below the surface which are crucial and which need urgent attending to. It is interesting that many liberalists who would reject Dostoevsky's beliefs would also reject Freud's negative conclusions concerning the human unhappiness engendered by the battle between civilization and the Id, with the latter's demand for gratification of all its manifold desires and impulses. However, the parallels between Dostoevsky and Freud obviously break down when we consider that whereas the former recognises that evil despite its irrational origins, is still a personal act of sin, which needs atonement and forgiveness, the latter is only interested in the socio-psychological reasons which cause humans to become unhappy, regressive and neurotic. This latter Freudian line of interest has been immensely influential on modern liberal Protestant thinking, with its whole tendency to turn away from the idea that evil is the product of a dark, demonic force. Negative toleration is fatally embedded for the liberals in their failure to accept this unpalatable truth. Nor can they accept that it is every single human being's responsibility to face up to the dark, in-growing flower of evil which blooms maliciously within the self.

The liberal Protestant would have no difficulty in quoting to the fundamentalist, St. John's gospel account of the woman caught in adultery, which displays the stark contrast between Christ's refusal to ratify the Mosaic law of condemnation, and the inflexible, attitude of the accusers. But there are two allusions to 'sin'; not only does Jesus admonish the woman to finish with her sinful ways (thus emphasising the radical change required of her) but before that he confronts the accusers with the disturbing challenge:

> "If any one of you is without sin, let him be the first to throw a stone at her".(13)

Perhaps the core problem of liberal toleration is the belief that most human beings -including liberals – are really quite decent and virtuous people. And all one needs to top up this inveterate decency is to toddle along to church either regularly or now and again; perhaps getting involved on rotas such as readings, flower arranging, stewarding and so forth. Yet until one looks deeply into the heart and starts to become critically aware of all that is there: the suppressed resentment, rage, bitterness, hurt, envy, jealousy, disappointment and perhaps incipient despair; until that point one is deluding oneself; one is living a pious lie. Moreover, unforgiveness is not merely restricted to meting out inexorable, legalistic punishments. Continual unforgiveness in the heart becomes itself a sin and thoughts can be full of criminality even though they may not be translated into actual criminal *acts*. Christ, as always, looks into the depths of the human condition, for it is there that evil has its birth, its fostering; it is there that it festers and grows and often imperceptibly permeates and distorts the human personality. Thus, Jesus instructs his disciples:

> "...the things that come out of the mouth come from the heart, and these make a man 'unclean'. For out of the heart comes evil thoughts, murder, adultery, sexual immorality, theft, false testimony, slander".
> (14)

It is precisely at this point where liberalism's tolerating attitude appears most superficial and conformist in its political correctness. Socrates dictum "know thyself" needs to be translated into Christian self-examination: "know thy sinful, Adam nature". The reality is that no human being is properly civilized in a Christian, or for that matter, a 'humanist' sense. As human beings we may exhibit politeness, kindness, sensitivity; we may also be immensely clever, knowledgeable, amusing, witty and in short, engaging personalities; but all this does not mean that we are free from significant psychological distortions which seriously infect some, if not all, of what is good in us. Returning to Freud, his great contribution, after all, is not to merely leave us with his case studies of patients suffering from neurosis, but rather to make us realise that all is not well in the state of Denmark; the so-called civilized westerners are very far from being perfectly integrated human beings. Life is actually a continuous battle in the personality structure, and it does not require so much as one thinks to develop crippling neuroses. In this sense, Freud appreciates in his humanistic way, that there is a deep besetting fallibility in the human condition, and unless one is prepared to register this fact and come to grips with it, life will merely be boxing with shadows and chasing after illusions. Freud obviously differs from the Judaic and Christian view of the human problem as being 'sin', but he has nevertheless helped explode the comfortable, self-satisfied (and quasi-religious) position of post-enlightenment 'progress'. As such, Freud may be seen as an unwitting ally of the ongoing work of Christ against Protestant liberal conformism.

As we have noted, a considerable debt is owed to the more vigorous methods of historical biblical exegesis, brought about by a more critically open-ended approach by many nineteenth and twentieth century scholars to the study of theology. Yet on the negative side, once again the weakness of liberalism (when it comes to Christ and his gospel), emanates from a misplaced emphasis on precisely this basic strength: the regard for knowledge. Of course in the context of exegesis and contextual study, it goes without saying that the pursuit of knowledge is fundamental. However, contemporary Christian liberal theology in varying degrees seems to be characterised by its own kind of cultic intellectuality, which consequently results in an increasing gulf between many theologians, clergy and the laity. The most extreme forms of such subjective exclusiveness effectively eclipses the incarnate, saving Word of God; namely, writings which reductively hold that salvation, as such, can now only reside in an open-eyed knowledge of de-construction; and that such knowledge, which rejects the supposedly dangerously outmoded doctrines of "classical Christianity" is the special prerequisite of more "enlightened" theologians.(15) Such a view positing a spurious "superior understanding" of the human situation naturally excludes the central basis of Christianity, which is concerned with finding salvation for one's soul.

Even when we come to milder, more mainstream liberal views on the gospel, we find that liberalist clergy and theologians tend to put an undue weight on the importance of Christ's role as teacher, often rendering the latter into little more than a western equivalent of Confucius (who himself never claimed to possessing any supernatural authority). But to shift most if not all the weight onto the gospel teachings of Christ is to eclipse the really central achievement of his *divine work,* namely, the reconciling sacrificial work of the atonement and its corresponding ratification in terms of the resurrection. But of course it is precisely liberalism's general agnosticism about transcendentalism which is responsible for negating the crucial centrality of both the atonement and the resurrection.

The atonement may be accepted on the basis of it being merely a great moral example of love, which flows out as a natural corollary of Christ's teaching, but there is an absolute recoiling from the idea that Jesus *chose* to die and indeed, had to die in order to wash away the burden of sin-guilt from the world. Likewise, the resurrection may be tolerated on the level of it being a cipher for the Christian's new Spirit-emancipated life, but the idea of a definite bodily resurrection (regardless of whether the new body is of a spiritual substance) is sneeringly dismissed as tantamount to believing in conjuring tricks.

The idea of forgiveness being achieved by voluntary, substitutionary punishment of someone completely innocent is anathema to many, if not most liberal theologians and clergy. But to dismiss the idea of Christ's atoning sacrifice is in effect to dismiss the cross, itself. Those who have opposed the atonement doctrine, suggesting it confounds God's love with juridical cruelty (16), fail to appreciate that there must be an *ultimate point* in which justice and love are reconciled by their fusing into one another. The cross universalises both the forgiveness and justice of God's love. It is through and only through this dramatic and indeed transcending fusion that salvation is opened up for all. Christ's death on the cross is therefore the crowning, cosmic summation and finish to all his work, which in his ministry of teaching and healing had of necessity only a localised scope. The cross cannot be compromised to suit liberal niceties. Only the death of God in Christ could bring in this final reconciling fusion between love and justice capable of bringing forth the promise of a clearance of guilt for all who accept Christ as Lord and Saviour. Who are mere men and women, even if they are gifted theologians, to say that God is not entitled to offer salvation through his own suffering in Christ on the cross?

The central Reformation tenet, that the believer has the right and autonomy of conscience to read and understand the gospel teachings for himself has undoubtedly finally led, albeit unwittingly, to theological liberalism exhorting Christ's teachings above his miraculous works of healing and redemption. Yet when John the Baptist (who was confined in prison and apparently having some doubts about Jesus) sent his followers to question Christ as to whether he really was the Messiah, the answer was thus:

> "Go back and report to John what you hear and see: The blind receive sight, the lame walk, those who have leprosy are cured, the deaf hear, the dead are raised, and the good news is preached to the poor".
> (17)

The emphasis is on the witness of the works. The radical nature of Christianity is not merely a change or enlightening of understanding in the head; rather it is a cleansing sweep through the whole being.

It is precisely because of liberalism's twin excessive emphases: Christ as merely a great moral teacher and the individual believer's autonomy, that many Protestants end up in a kind of theological bubble, unable to connect fully with other Christians. In this sense liberalism ends up in fragmenting

Christ's church. Everyone has their separate interpretations. There can be no real coming together of a universal Christian brotherhood. The signal failure of liberal Protestantism is its isolationism which is responsible for the failure to engage in building up the earthly community of Christ's body. Whereas the fundamentalists get lost in an objectivity rendered redundant by an obsessive literalism, the liberalist gets bogged down in a vague subjectivity. Forgotten is God's will and purpose as it was manifested in the objective events of Christ's life, death and resurrection. Forgotten are the objective facts of the conversion and ministry of St. Paul. So too, the concrete acts of other apostles become irrelevant and of no significance. But unless it is seen that God has objectively entered into human history and is *still working* in history, Christianity will have no relevance to human solidarity and the building of Christ's Church on earth. Liberalism in this above sense of wilful forgetfulness is not Christianity at all.

CHAPTER 3

FAILURE OF FUNDAMENTALISM AND LIBERALISM

The two previous chapters have attempted to show that despite many important and constructive qualities, both fundamentalism and liberalism end up by being seriously vitiated through various defective features and tendencies germane to each of their outlooks. Before we move on to a consideration of what the "gospel of risk" really is as evidenced by the *New Testament* records let us attempt to summarise and fully understand the reasons why both fundamentalism and liberalism have ultimately failed in their respective tasks of conveying the authentic gospel to our contemporary society.

Fundamentalism espouses itself as a theology of *triumph*, maintaining that Christianity should be nothing but a release of continuous celebratory joy. Liberalism is in effect a theology of *caution*, with the implication that Christianity should be carefully gone into, being continually evaluated and up-dated so to make it supposedly relevant and acceptable to the hard-nosed scientific and technocratic age. Fundamentalism revels in the omnipotent God, and his Son, the latter who will come probably very soon at a mighty trumpet blast, triumphantly riding on a cloud with legions of angels, bringing in the "rapture," where those who are of Christ will be immediately taken up into the bliss of heaven. By contrast, cold-eyed liberalism tends to be sceptical about anything that might be construed as supernatural. Thus it weights the emphasis on the humanity of Christ and is less concerned with proclaiming the triumph of the resurrection as the latter obviously involves belief which stretches beyond mere human boundaries.

If fundamentalism fails because it distorts Christ's gospel into a kind of neo-legalistic reward and punishment scheme, drastically reducing the width and inclusiveness of God's love, then liberalism fails equally through its in-built scepticism and its procedure of endless qualifications which seriously emasculates the gospel of good news. So on the one hand the failure is of presenting Christ's gospel as a kind of grand tea party for all those who have dramatically stepped into heaven by one supposedly decisive act of faith; on the other hand the failure is of failing to suggest that there is any heavenly banquet at all; that we should not make too much noise about Christianity as it might be construed that we are too exclusive, intolerant and excitable. The fundamentalist failure is primarily one of narrowness born of simplistic assumptions while the liberal failure is primarily one of dilution – in the desire to be politically correct and thus tolerant to all, the truth and power of the gospel is accordingly diluted into something which will not cause any offence.

To take fundamentalism first: why then is it wrong in putting all the emphasis on Christianity as a theology of joy and triumphalism for its adherents? The liberal would say that the emphatic emphasis on joy is simplistic and does no justice to the fact that the world is both a complex and an unhappy place and moreover, the human personality even more complex in its unfulfilled yearnings and psychological workings. The liberal would also say that triumphalism smacks dangerously of self-conceit and is opposed to Christ's creed of humility, service and self-sacrifice to others. And such criticism goes to the heart of the matter. For instance, the criticism of spiritual smugness is fully backed up by St. Paul's words to the Corinthians:

> "We do not dare to classify or compare ourselves with some who commend themselves... they are not wise. We, however, will not boast beyond proper limits... But, "Let him who boasts boast in the Lord". For it is not the one who commends himself who is approved, but the one whom the Lord commends". (1)

Triumphalism, which is connected to the category of boasting is necessarily a limited vision. It is essentially a bland Manichean vision of black versus white, good versus evil.

It is significant that fundamentalists refer back to the *Old Testament* for much of their imagery and aggressive outlook. Generally speaking, the Judaic outlook was essentially triumphalistic in terms of the prevalent messianic belief concerning the eventual destruction of Israel's enemies, ensuring a final and complete geographical, political and economic hegemony for the "chosen people". However, there were the great prophets, who besides continually criticising Israel's rulers and people for their hypocrisy, greed and injustice, did in fact strongly attest to Jehovah's ultimate concern to stretch out his love to peoples of all nations.(2) Even as far back as the *Book of Genesis* we find the great promise given to Abraham:

"You will be the father of many nations."(3)

But such words and intimations given by the prophets that foreign races could also receive God's blessing through, for instance, their corporate acts of repentance (4), did not cut much ice with the Jewish authorities. The rest of the known ancient world was generally put into a lower order of importance. Current Anglo-American fundamentalism psychologically and politically mirrors the (generally) belligerent nationalistic approach of ancient Judaism. Tragically, the fundamentalist is more often than not looking with Judaic rather than Christian eyes at the world. Like many ancient Israelite leaders and those of today's hard line militaristic core of Zionists, the fundamentalist is equating salvation with materialism: territory, and all the trappings of political and economic power.

For the contemporary fundamentalist it is hardly too great an exaggeration to say everything hinges on the State of Israel, which as far as the former is concerned still represents in all senses 'the chosen people,' having an apparently divine mandate to take back (ruthlessly, if necessary) Palestinian land and lord it over those who mistakenly oppose her aims. In adopting this localised view of 'Israel', fundamentalism is guilty of de-spiritualising Christ's gospel. Ironically, the fundamentalist puts himself or herself almost back into the same position as those who opposed Christ during his earthly ministry. For just as Jesus was severely hampered by those who espoused materialistic beliefs of a militaristic, all conquering Messiah, rendering freedom in terms of land, wealth and political power, so too is his gospel today confronted with fundamentalism's pro-Zionism. A bizarre contradiction is evidenced as a result of this pro-Zionism. The fundamentalist loudly proclaims that the only way to God is through Jesus Christ, categorically dismissing the other world faiths. However, the fundamentalist fails to see or acknowledge that the Judaic religion, like other world religions, also continues to reject Christ as Messiah, as incarnate Saviour.

Israelites and gentiles: From Christ onwards it is imperative that we understand these nouns in a spiritual, not localised, restrictive politico-geographical sense. The fundamentalist failure to think in terms of a spiritual Israel lies at the heart of a failure to understand the enormous changes Christ wrought in terms of the enlargement of the concept of 'the chosen people'. It is not a case of liberalist Christians rejecting the *Old Testament* by rejecting the Jews as God's 'chosen people', it is rather a case that the concept of a 'chosen people' has become expanded to include not just one nation but all nations. St. Paul goes so far as even to enlarge in spiritual terms the concept of what it meant to be an authentic Jew:

> "A man is not a Jew if he is only one outwardly, nor is circumcision merely outward and physical. No, a man is a Jew if he is one inwardly; and circumcision is circumcision of the heart, by the Spirit, not by the written code". (5)

The fact is that all who accept Christ in humble, non-legalistic faith are true *spiritual Israelites*, and it is those who deny Christ's gospel and work against his ways of forgiving and self-sacrificial love who are *spiritual Gentiles*. The whole fundamentalist problem, which includes its lamentable, restrictive conformist attitudes, is precisely a failure to transpose materialist terms into spiritual terms. Early in Jesus' earthly ministry, a warning had been sounded through his words to the Samaritan woman at the well:

> "...a time is coming and has now come when the true worshippers will worship the Father in spirit and truth, for they are the kind of worshippers the Father seeks. God is spirit, and his worshippers must worship in spirit and in truth". (6)

Such is God's kingdom. And if God is spirit it follows that he cannot be wholly located in one race or contained in geographical locations, no matter how much significance they may have had or still have.

The fundamentalist's rejection of the *New Israel* as being a slur on the original 'chosen people' arises from a signal failure to really grasp the profound nature of Christ's ministry and the new covenant which he established. Fundamentalism tries to live in both the old and new covenants, but this is impossible, for the new has superseded the old:

> "No-one sews a patch of unshrunk cloth on an old garment. If he does, the new piece will pull away from the old, making the tear worse. And no-one pours new wine into old wineskins. If he does, the wine will burst the skins and both the wine and the wineskins will be ruined. No, he pours new wine into new wineskins". (7)

The old covenant can no longer contain within its narrowly specified Mosaic, nationhood laws the new enlargement to the kingdom which Christ ushers in by his ministry and supremely through his death and resurrection. The new wineskin of Christ's covenant is capable of containing the new enlarged kingdom, and this is precisely what the old covenant is now *incapable* of doing. The fundamentalists are thus living in a contradiction by trying to cling to the old covenant, which was designed for one single nation, and yet at the same time boldly claiming the promises of the new covenant which is designed to include all nations. Either one really accepts what Christ has done to enlarge the heavenly kingdom or one is self-constrained to live in a reductive, prejudiced world which flies completely in the face of Jesus' assertion that "God is spirit". If God is spirit then his people must themselves live by the principle of spirit where there are no longer the materialistic boundaries which mark off a one-nation faith. The two greatest Jewish apostles, despite starting from the localised vision of a nationalistic Israel, came to realise most forcibly the new basis of the covenant Christ had wrought by his own blood:

> "...God does not show favouritism but accepts men from every nation who fear him and do what is right". (8)

So declares St. Peter, and in his letter to the Romans, St. Paul again stresses that the phrase: 'chosen people' must now be interpreted in a much wider and extensive light:

> "For there is no difference between Jew and Gentile – the same Lord is Lord of all and richly blesses all who call on him". (9)

But the fundamentalist in his crass materialism would have it that there *is* a difference. And in blindly maintaining this difference the fundamentalist effectually resists the full releasing power of the new covenant which offers the possibility of reconciliation, understanding and peace among nations.

In considering the fundamentalist's idea that joy should be a continuous feature of the Christian life, the first thing to be said is that the problem hinges upon a false conception of what Christian joy actually is. The fundamentalist seems to believe that Christian joy is bound up entirely with the human emotions. Again there is the failure to view 'joy' as primarily an inward, spiritual attribute or experience. The danger of needing to be always manifesting exuberant spirits to confirm one's depth of faith is something equivalent to St. Paul's admonition about the danger of being only an outwardly circumcised Jew. The controlled harmony of inner joy is a very different thing from the exhibitionism of emotional protestations of love for Jesus which are the standard thing one comes across in fundamentalist services and meetings. Much of what goes on in such gatherings and rallies merely results in people working themselves into a state of cooked-up emotionalism, which they sadly mistake for real Christian 'joy'. But spiritual 'joy' in reality constitutes a profound state of equilibrium. Precisely because of that profound anchoring state of being, it is possible to experience a momentary liberation from the innumerable torments of an imperfect piecemeal existence, and this in itself will amount to a kind of mild ecstasy.

A real inward harmony, a real Christian joy is of necessity something which cannot be pinned down, measured and brought out on display as if it were perfectly in our control. It can only be continually sought for in prayer, obedience and in the doing of Christ's work in the world. The liberal's caution at this point is better founded when compared to the pugnacious over-confidence of the fundamentalist.

But let us in our analysis of fundamentalist conformism consider another important element: love. Fundamentalist services and meetings are characterised by many repetitive songs all centred in declaring love for Jesus and this again borders on the literalism of wanting to touch him and so forth.

Again, the liberal would be right in seeing that the fundamentalist is guilty of de-spiritualising things and therefore of missing the point. And the point being that the real love for Jesus is in a loving responsiveness towards others. Christ did not want to be worshipped, he rebukes the rich young man who addresses him as "Good teacher":

"No-one is good – except God alone" (10).

Paradoxically the true love of Christ is expressed by a caring, self-sacrificial love towards others rather than directly to himself. And this is the meaning of the sheep and goats parable (11). Christian love must have practical issue or it is not Christian love at all. Praise on its own is not enough. Despite all the grand protestations of being alive in the Spirit, fundamentalism fails to reach out and help people with all their various problems which emanate from psychological instabilities and a world where there are increasingly less and less certainties to anchor to. Fundamentalism tragically fails to continue the liberating work of Christ. Conformism and liberation do not mix. The overriding failure of fundamentalism, finally, is one of failing to engage in the fullness of the modern world's expanded reality. The fundamentalist at bottom is a reactionary, a person striving to conform all the world into his own image. But his own image is inflexible and hopelessly outmoded and therefore does not sufficiently reflect the Saviour's image. The infinitely resourceful love of Christ has room to meet lovingly with the problems of the whole world, whereas fundamentalism has already pre-decided the rules and regulations of love in its snug but closed universe.

In assessing the failure of Christian liberalism we come to the opposite tendencies to triumph and joy, namely, caution and scepticism. From the onset it is important to remember that not only does Christian liberalism feed in off the new developments in biblical research, but that its theologians (as well as many educated lay people) also feed in off the new developments and ideas stemming from both the sciences and humanities. There is therefore a lot brewing in the pot! But the new ideas brewing in the pot, whether emanating from theology, the sciences or humanism, tend on the whole to breed the reductive atmosphere conducive of over-cautious and sceptical belief. It is of course right to display caution in its proper context, but the fundamentalists have some grounds for claiming that liberalism is only engaging with a dry abstraction rather than with the living God. The former might also have good grounds for claiming that if you continue to cast doubts on scriptural authority, there will eventually be no gospel left worth proclaiming. Certainly, in Protestant liberalism there seems to be an ongoing battle between the biblical God and the god of post-rationalism, with the former often coming out of the contest in worse shape than the latter.

The truth is that with regard to the contemporary sciences and humanities, wherever one looks concerning the key ideas and developments, there is ultimately a nihilistic view of life and the universe. For instance a brain scientist such as Francis Crick claims that human beings are no more than conglomerations of neurons and Richard Dawkins, the British ethologist, devolves everything down to his 'selfish gene' principle. When we turn to the humanities things are not much brighter. Let us take examples from three differing fields. In the so-called fine-arts, conceptual art and the pernicious doctrine of "anything can be art" result merely in fatuous images and banal 'installations'. Likewise, in much English poetry from Larkin and Hughes onwards, there is little but a barely contained hatred towards the human existential situation.(12) Turning to post-modern drama, what is primarily found is the extensive influence of the reductive and pessimistic Samuel Beckett, which has helped set the overriding basis of many other playwrights such as Harold Pinter. Because of Protestant liberalism's openness to cultural influences, all this type of minimalism and negativity is feeding into it and accordingly producing distorted ideas of Christianity.

The fundamentalist fear is precisely against being too open to outside influences. The reasoning goes that once you make a chink in the sheep fold it will become bigger and bigger. There is considerable truth in this as can be seen for instance by the inroads of the permissive society. Also, in more direct Christian terms, we can see how latitude has led to the blatant heresies of liberalism in its extreme modes. In the 1960's Bishop John Robinson denied that God should have an image. (13) By the 1970's onwards, such theologians as Don Cupid were through the media as well as books, denying much more than this.(14) But again it is important to note that whereas Robinson was getting his leading ideas from Teutonic theologians such as Bonhoeffer, Bultmann and Tillich, who were deeply believing Christians, Cupid's ideas were coming from secular intellectual sources. And this secular influence is a main reason for the extreme basis of much contemporary Protestant liberal thought.

Taking Don Cupid as a significant example, we find in his works mainly references to secular rather than theological thinkers. For instance, among the many secular references in *The Long Legged Fly*, there is an approving reference to the philosopher, Richard Rorty's view "that everything – the world, morality, language, truth, man – must be completely 'de-divinized'"(15). When one follows up this reference, looking into Rorty's thought, one is confronted with an outlook which sees only "...a world of blind, contingent, mechanical forces".(16) And for Rorty, as no doubt for Don Cupid and other ultra-liberal Protestants, basically appearance is 'reality', with nothing beyond it. Existence – appearance – is in fact no more than language:

> "To say that truth is not out there is simply to say that where there are no sentences there is no truth". (17)

Language is the only reality. If this is the case, good and evil is merely a question of the way language happens to be shaped. Where, then, does this leave the power of the human spirit – and thus human imaginative creativity? To say that truth is no more than language is to say that the contingent is everything, and apparently such a position would be quite acceptable to Don Cupid. In fact in the latter author's note to *The Long Legged Fly*, he has no great qualms about our "age of thoroughgoing reductionism" but instead maintains that like an insect known as the "pond skater", we must make "a world out of ...minimal materials"(18). So, we are left with only a pond-surface reality. The "good news" of Cupid's gospel is that there is nothing below the surface; that we must therefore become adroit, existential pond-skating insects. Must we assume that human beings are nothing more than a very sophisticated breed of thinking insects? The logical upshot of Cupid's position is to give credence to today's unconsciously held (by most people) doctrine of existential materialism. Such a view holds that the world is absurd because it has no final or absolute meaning but we humans can give it some meaning by the way we live our lives. The only truth (or truths) is what we produce in the relative context of our own personal lives. For Cupid, it is up to us to construct our own subjective world out of the rubble left by scientific and philosophical reductionism. Yet Cupid gainsays such a minimalist and pointless world precisely by suggesting that it is possible for us to create our own relative versions of meaning (and therefore truth of some degree); thus he is merely moving into another variation of the old utopian: "man is the measure".

But it is well to remember Dr. Johnson's words:

> "...the nature of things is not alterable by our conduct. We cannot make truth; it is our business only to find it". (19)

That is to say, existential materialism is only an adopted attitude. It is not truth at all, but merely what suits an attitude which has certain self-centred inclinations.

Even when we turn back to Bishop Robinson, who still deeply believed Christianity to be a powerful force (as long as it was portrayed in what he viewed as a relevant way to the postmodern world), we see the fatal roots of liberal caution and scepticism. It is not merely a justified rejection of the image of a benevolent, bearded God in a three-decker universe, rather it is a far deeper distrust about the whole transcendental basis of Christianity which motivates Robinson and particularly so in his book, *Honest to God*. But is Robinson honest to Christ? Is there nothing transcendental about Jesus Christ becoming incarnate in human flesh? Is Christ the ultimate revelation of God or is he not? These are questions which are not convenient for Robinson to deal with. The focus is purely on one half of the Chalcedon formula – Christ's transcendent perfection as a man, not as perfect God. Robinson, here is heavily indebted to Bonhoeffer's influential Christological coinage: "the man for others"(20), and in fact uses that phrase as title for one of his key chapters in *Honest to God*. In the crystallisation of his thoughts, Robinson was also significantly influenced by Ronald Gregor Smith's book: *The New Man*, which elaborates the latter's concern to do away with the classical Christian concept of otherworldly transcendence. The core of Gregor Smith's argument is well represented by the following extract, which itself is largely dependent on Bonhoeffer's fragmentary prison writings:

> "Our relationship to God is not a religious relationship to a supreme being, absolute in power and goodness, which is a spurious conception of transcendence, but a new life for others, through participation in the being of God".(21)

But here is the problem! If our relationship to God – to Christ – is not to a supreme being, what does this make God, or turn him into? Is St. Paul totally mistaken, then, to view Christ as Lord of the universe?

> "For by him all things were created: things in earth and on earth, visible and invisible, whether thrones or powers or rulers or authorities; all things were created by him and for him. He is before all things and in him all things hold together".(22)

Such a Pauline view is a vision far in excess of Gregor Smith's view of the earthbound, humanitarian Christ, who can only help us by means of serving others and being defeated – being crucified by his enemies. Now, while this view of Christ helping us even to the extent of his human suffering and weakness upon the cross (which Bonhoeffer brilliantly touched upon in his prison writings) is very relevant and liberating, the danger is that one can forget the other half of the equation – namely, the victorious divine Christ, who having triumphantly finished his earthly work, in symbolical terms ascends to the Father to sit at his right hand, interceding for all those who carry on his work on earth. Christ, indeed, is "the man for others", but also he represents something even far greater; namely, he represents a great liberating force of transcendence which is right at the very heart of the universe. Either there is this centre of divine power which mysteriously holds in place the whole universe, with all its diverse life forms, or there is not, and in which case we are left with the wonderful, historical Christ, but a Christ who is exclusively confined to humanity and therefore robbed of the full status of his divine *logos*. Thus, again, Gregor Smith:

> "Christ is not a heavenly fantasy, or a *tour de force* on the part of an inaccessible otherness; but he is the givenness of transcendence, he is transcendence in its only accessible form, namely, in a human life in human history, in the one world which all men share as the place of their destiny". (23)

One could immediately argue that "otherness" was not necessarily inaccessible to Old Testament prophets such as Isaiah and Ezekiel; nor has the risen (non-earthly) Christ's "otherness" been "inaccessible" to the countless Christian visionaries and saints down the succeeding ages. But moreover, there is a confusion in Gregor Smith's idea of the incarnate Christ. True, Christ becomes accessible through becoming human, but what of the mystery of incarnation itself? Does not Gregor Smith forget that even though the incarnation makes God into a human person, at the same time this emptying of divinity is itself a supreme example of a transcendence which is utterly "other" in terms of its supernatural overleaping of all human laws and processes?

But how can we gain benefits if God, Christ and the Holy Spirit are less than the supreme, Trinitarian being? And what exactly is grace if bereft of its supernatural basis? Gregor Smith's position (and for that matter Robinson's) must in its logic devolve down into some kind of enhanced humanism. Is there not a danger here in one sense of merely a quibble on words, namely, that of the supposed need to free transcendence from the notions of the supernatural? Are not Gregor Smith and Robinson merely transposing Nietzsche's superman into a Christian superman; in other words, a superman who has subsumed God's supernatural "otherness" into a personal religious transcendence? What is going on here is precisely the attempt to de-divinise Christ – and therefore God. Christ is not a God for others but a man for others. But if Christ is not God then the incarnation is void, the cross becomes transcendent only as an example and the resurrection is merely a subjective confirmation of the power of Jesus' example. The issue comes down to whether Christ is God or not. If he is not, then the way is paved for the transformation of Christianity into a new humanism which increasingly has no sense or indeed need of the dialectic between Creator and creature. It makes possible a new de-divinised theology which consequently treats Christ as "one of us" who "made good". An inverted form of adoptionism, where we humans adopt Christ into our human fold because he did so well as a human being! Here we can only have a radically dis-empowered Christ, who can hardly be the triumphant 'yes' to all God's great promises to his believers.(24) Nor can this be the Christ who made the great claim that his incarnation purpose was that those who heeded his call would receive a new life brimming with fullness.(25) But a de-divinised theology can only result in a Christianity with the plug pulled out; a counterfeit Christianity because it is no longer plugged into the divine source of transcending power.

The expressions and language of the Chalcedon Definition (451) may now be archaic in certain respects, but if we are to continue to believe in the Trinity, its basic premise concerning Christ: "true God, true man" must still hold good. Without the divine sense of Christ's Godly power Christianity could not possibly have been the source of inextinguishable strength and comfort for the countless known and unknown saints and martyrs all over the globe who have at various times striven against the barbarous cruelties and injustices of those who organise and rule the world. Thus, the true devout Christian's life is still, as always, "hidden with Christ in God"(26), and this very Pauline phrase evokes the undergirding supernatural transcendence of grace. Such power is clearly not of the world. It is no good pretending that such mysterious power is merely mumbo-jumbo, for without such power the Christian would have no new life and certainly no ability to be a person for others. Human transcendence does not come out of itself, just as Christ's transcendence did not come out of his own human resources; rather it arises out of the supernatural transcendence of grace which is a gift given to all those who are prepared to persevere in obedience and loving communion with God. In fact all the major Christian terms of reference are soaked in supernaturalism. The Lord's Supper, for example, could hardly be called an act of merely human transcendence! Its whole essence is the breaking in of the divine into the created world of material things and human beings.

> "Glory be to the Father, and to the Son and to the Holy Ghost; As it was in the beginning, is now and ever shall be: world without end".

Are we to play down or deny the above words found in the

Common Prayer Book, which celebrate the time-transcending 'otherness' of the Trinity? Moreover, the final point of Christ's gospel goes beyond the ethic of 'being for others' (which is a means not an end) to the *salvation of souls*. Salvation is ultimately bound up with the mystery of God's unfathomable grace. The mystery includes Jesus' cryptic words to Nicodemus about the need to be "born again"(27) and St. Paul's assertion that:

"...if anyone is in Christ, he is a new creation"... (28)

Salvation is *being in Christ* (29), it is not just about being a good neighbour or being forgiven and redeemed (important as these things are); it is essentially about that most intimate of relationships, that of living one's whole life *through* Christ; living with him and for him in the power of the Holy Spirit.

"I tell you the truth" Jesus says to the repentant thief hanging beside him, "today you will be with me in paradise".(30) Presumably such words would only constitute a form of subjective encouragement when evaluated by the liberalist who would slavishly follow the new doctrine of worldly transcendence. What is missing here is the failure to see the sheer releasing power of God's word in Christ. To be with Christ is to be with God; it is to transcend by faith even the worst that can happen to you – even to transcend the horror and ignominy of death on a cross. Protestant liberalism at its worst (that is when it becomes over weighted with humanism) is in danger of forgetting what Christianity is for.

Concerning the general problem of modern disbelief, C.S. Lewis, in 1948 wrote:

> "The ancient man approached God (or even the gods) as the accused person approaches his judge. For the modern man the roles are reversed. He is the judge: God is in the dock". (31)

These words could be well applied to much of the theological, liberal establishment. There is a fundamental scepticism towards the idea of a Trinitarian God who is a miraculous Creator, Saviour and enabling Spirit. The disillusionment following two catastrophic world wars, the holocaust, an escalating production of nuclear weapons; environmental calamities, famine, the de-humanizing greed and injustice of Capitalism, seem often in the liberal Protestant consciousness to put God "in the dock"

If God is there at all he is there to be somehow blamed, not to be praised. Christ, "the man for others" is, as "one of us," acceptable because he suffered all the injustices which are liable to human beings. But the risen and triumphant second person of the Trinity is unacceptable precisely because the very notion of transcendence overleaps all the neat logical steps of humanism, and this therefore, for the liberal theologian, makes Christ suspect because in this respect he cannot be "one of us". Moreover, it can be seen that with their unbalanced application of Bonhoeffer's fragmentary writings, Gregor Smith and Robinson have helped to further liberal theology's already damaging split-off between immanence and transcendence.

For immanence, taken by itself without transcendence, leads to the Feuerbachian position which is in fact human self-immanence. With theologians such as Don Cupid this idea is carried through to its logical conclusion, where immanence is nothing other than a principle of personal subjectivity in terms of self-realization.

Because of its sceptical and cautious attitudes (which emanate from its ultra-rationalistic, enlightenment basis, rather than from the *New* Testament) liberal theology lives under a number of contradictions. One cannot help, for instance, feel that liberal theology – even though its milieu is largely composed of an ongoing negative revisionism and deconstruction – still lives in another sense under the large shadow of Renaissance optimism: "man is the measure". Yet twined with this one also cannot but feel that many liberal Protestant thinkers are weighed down by a secret fear that Freud was perhaps right when he concluded that religion at best is merely a necessary fiction.(32). Thus liberalism is enmeshed in a shadowy, contradictory world of false hope and false fear, neither of which can possibly reflect the true liberating gospel of Christ.

At the same time it is clear that fundamentalism also suffers from serious contradictions. It preaches the optimism of the gospel of "good news", yet by a consistent failure to rid itself of a negative attitude to the world concerning those who are "unsaved", it turns into (in this respect) a narrow and self-regarding sectarian religion. Fundamentalism preaches love and yet what it so often practises falls far short of Christ's ideals. And this is because real Christian love demands risk; that is to say, an authentic, unconditional openness of self-giving. In this key sense, fundamentalism is not a gospel of risk. Liberalism's concept of Christian love is more magnanimous, but it fails to take into account the sheer indwelling depth of human evil; thus its view of love is posited on the unrealistic basis of a supposed inherent human goodness. Accordingly, the basis is one of ethical casuistry (that of looking at matters from a situational context) with the assumption that psychological and social rehabilitation programmes – alone – are the way of healing and therefore of dealing with evil and its effects. This naive way of looking at evil purely in terms of various types of psychological and environmental causal processes, seriously overlooks the Biblical attestation that human beings after Eden are *lapsarian beings*; that is they each carry within them, in varying degrees, a distorted human condition which is beyond any mere human repairing. The only real attitude of a human being to God is enshrined in Isaiah's painful visionary experience of being called to prophecy in the temple:

> "Woe to me!" I cried. "I am ruined! For I am a man of unclean lips, and I live among a people of unclean lips, and my eyes have seen the King, the Lord Almighty". (33)

Or that of the publican in the temple who:
> "...beat his breast and said, 'God, have mercy on me, a sinner'. (34)

In both examples human self-esteem is completely shattered

by an authentic encounter or communion with the Creator. But it is precisely the cultivation of self-esteem (or in Jungian psychological terms, "self-integration") which is the leading ethical element of contemporary Christian liberalism. The implication being that the power for goodness can only emanate from the combination of human self-control and self-assuredness. However, if there is no need for a through-going and life-changing repentance, but instead one can humanly (or spiritually?) develop by means of an ongoing self-realization process, there would appear to be little scope for the transcendent Christ of glory, whom the disciples, Peter and John, caught a momentary but awe-inspiring vision of on the Mount of Transfiguration.

Perhaps because Protestant liberalism is so wary of the idea of an absolute faith-commitment, it misunderstands and indeed despises the thrusting optimism of fundamentalism. Equally, perhaps it is also because fundamentalism is so enmeshed in a "theology of glory" that it completely misunderstands Christian liberalism, seeing the latter only as a negative intellectual brake on the enthusiasm required for proclaiming the "good news". What is perhaps so sad in this mutual reciprocation of misunderstandings is that both these 'isms throw away the chance to learn what is of true value in the other and thereby each remains a severely diminished extrapolation of the true Christian gospel.

CHAPTER 4

THE GOSPEL OF RISK

Conservatism in its own absolute sphere is merely repression and oppression. Liberalism in its own absolute sphere is merely licence and laxity. Radicalism in its own absolute sphere devolves down to anarchy and terrorism. Conservatism without balances and checks is authority which brooks or admits no contradictions to its ruling policies. Liberalism without any constraints paves the way to hedonism. Radicalism without any proper controls leads ultimately to the suicide bomber. Any proper civilisation involving the free expression of human rights has always needed to be based on a pragmatic blend between the elements of conservatism, liberalism and to a lesser extent (but still importantly) radicalism. True civilisation exists in-between extremes. Christianity, as is life itself, is a mixture of conservative, liberal and radical elements. But in Christianity the conservative and liberal elements are interconnected, penetrated and illumined by the radicalism of the supernatural power of God's grace. And this radicalism in its divine transcendence is entirely different to human forms of radicalism.

Christianity concerns the Kingdom of Heaven, and in this transcendent sense it concerns the one and only true everlasting civilisation – the civilisation of the Creator, Father God. The Kingdom is the perfect spiritual and therefore radical civilisation that encompasses and embraces all nations within its realm. But to preach the gospel appertaining to this, as yet imperfectly realised – and therefore largely hidden Kingdom – is the gospel of risk, because as St. John tells us:

> "...the whole world is under the control of the evil one". (1)

St. John means by the " whole world" the human heart in its universally fallen and corrupted state. Here, then, is the underlying basis of the massive opposition to Christ's gospel, which made it the gospel of risk when Jesus proclaimed and acted it out, and which still today makes it a gospel of risk for anyone who is prepared to be a true Christian disciple.

From a cursory glance it could be argued that Christianity is conservative insofar as it claims that Jesus Christ is the only way to the Father:

> "Salvation is found in no-one else, for there is no other name under heaven given to men by which we must be saved".(2)

It can be also seen that the gospel enjoins a magnanimity of forgiveness – "seventy times seven" (3) which seems somewhat akin to liberalist toleration. And regarding radicalism, we note the radical, absolutist nature of Christ's injunction to would-be disciples to take up their cross (4). But what we further find when we study the gospels is how integrated within each other the elements of conservatism, liberalism and radicalism actually are. Let us consider some examples.

The action of Christ clearing the money lenders out of the temple at Jerusalem could be seen as both a conservative and radical action. It could be construed a conservative action insofar as Christ, by driving out the money lenders, is re-claiming back the proper reverential purpose for the temple. The action could also be construed as radical in that Christ as a 'marked man' by the authorities is doing a daring public action in driving out those doing business in the temple. And not only that, for Christ is implying he has a special, even divine authority to do so. Christ quotes to the people there verses from the prophets Isaiah and Jeremiah, which he sees as being illuminated and therefore fulfilled by his own angry, violent reaction :

> "It is written", he said to them, "My house will be called a house of prayer, but you are making it a 'den of robbers'". (5).

In this doubly defiant action of clearing the temple and of quoting the prophets as implying his own divine authority, Christ, through his own Spirit-filled zeal (which far surpasses the formalistic religiosity of his opponents), is putting himself at risk from those in power who already hate him. At the same time his action points dramatically to the need to 'conserve' the sacred function of God's uniquely designated "house of prayer". Thus, in this particular gospel episode, the two elements of radicalism and conservatism are intimately interwoven together, and in fact illuminate and compliment each other. Perhaps one should remember here that one of the great mysterious paradoxes of the gospel is:

"...that in all things God works for the good of those who love him..."(6).

In Christ, particularly, we see an amazing integration of opposites which help to produce a revolutionary gospel of power, justice and love. That is why it can never be merely a gospel in a narrowed down political sense.

Let us take one further example to again demonstrate the way seemingly opposing elements often fuse together in the gospels. Consider the parable found in Luke's gospel of the Prodigal Son. (7) Here the liberal element would seem to reside in the father's open hearted, unconditional forgiveness of his errant but contrite son. The elder son is aggrieved at this, viewing it as easy forgiveness to his younger brother. The parable points up his false kind of conservative attitude (because mean-spirited and legalistic) which could be summarised as: "I have been the loyal, steadfast one, consistently attending scrupulously to my duties. There should be none of this liberal push-button forgiveness to such a waster". But the father's attitude of unbounding, joyful forgiveness at receiving his lost son back again (which of course mirrors the Creator's attitude to those who return to him in repentance) could be construed radical, for there was far more reason to give the prodigal a sound punishment for the thoughtless way he squandered his inheritance. But even again, we could say that the father's attitude also demonstrates a true conservatism, that is to say he acts with a true conserving love for the unity of his family. In fully re-instating his errant son the father re-affirms the unity of his family and this amounts to a positive and indeed loving form of conservatism. The prodigal's contrite return home is itself a form of positive conservatism (involving the realisation that the good things of life were really after all bound up with home and family) which is in marked contrast to his former excessive liberality. So here we see an intricate interweaving of all three elements. The net result is that Christ's gospel is a gospel of opposites and their reconciliation. That is why it is both a gospel based on clear-eyed realism and a gospel of hope in its "good news" of salvation. The risk is in bringing to light all the tensions and problems of fallen humanity and then being prepared to enter in the midst of all this wreckage and offer forgiveness and peace. Now we have noted examples of particular contextual usages of features of conservatism (what is rightly fundamental to maintaining a real unity) and liberalism (what is rightly liberal in its generousness), it is perhaps appropriate once again to repeat that it is not a matter of denying fundamentalist and liberalist elements but rather a case of seeing how the gospel properly integrates and uses them. But now let us turn more fully to the question of what the gospel of risk actually constitutes.

It must first be asserted that everything Christ did concerning those whom he encountered in their various needs involved a setting free. Yet it was precisely Christ's practice of setting people free from their oppressions of bodily and mental illness, their sins and weaknesses, which caused him to be at risk. It can only be the greatest tragic irony, that in giving others liberty from various oppressions, Christ was ultimately undermining his own personal liberty. The fallen world is a place of bondage; it is a place of necessity, a place more or less in various degrees dominated by the "master-slave" dialectic. To attempt to change this worldly pattern of authoritarian exploitation and its concomitant servitude is, to say the least, hazardous. But Christ's project of bringing in the Kingdom necessarily involved bringing reformation and freedom to tax collectors, harlots, demoniacs and other despised members and outcasts of society. The logical effect of liberating these people from their various constrictions was in a sense to send shudders of fear and hatred down the spines of those in authority, including powerful groups such as Priests, Pharisees and Sadducees. For any rabbinical teacher merely to take an interest in marginalized and supposedly 'wicked' people was to be bending against the socially perceived 'norms'. But to *actively* help these people and in effect to rehabilitate them as citizens was seen to be something as akin to fermenting unrest and an unsettling of the *status quo*.

Secondly, it must be asserted that although Christ was carrying out a project involving healing people from their various burdens (whether bodily, mental or spiritual) under the auspices of the Father, at the same time what was being made manifest was the spontaneous, unconditional outflow of God's love for *all* his created beings. Christ's ministry had its definite purpose – its divine mandate of reconciling humankind to God – but within that overarching aim (which culminates in the cross and resurrection) there was displayed a radically new vision of a loving, Father God, whose actions of love are not limited merely to the holy, the righteous, but in fact also encompass those who are the unlovely – the lost and the greatly strayed. Here was something much more than the scribal and pharisaic Mosaic religion, based on the tedious impossibility of fulfilling every tiny detail of the law. In such a religion the ruling idea tended to be that one must be *morally acceptable* to God and this could only be really achieved through a righteousness in keeping the minutia of the law. Such a continuous striving to keep the Mosaic law (with its ever increasing, 'protective fence' of added stipulations) was seen as what earned the merit which enabled one to be righteousness enough to be acceptable to God. Against this, Christ in his parables of the lost sheep, lost coin and prodigal son, gives us radically new pictures of a God who actively and with infinite love is seeking the lost.(8) The love of God through these parabolic pictures is thus more like a great sweeping searchlight than a reward for the arduous keeping to the detailed points of various regulations. And Christ demonstrates in his own ministry that he himself is that great arc of light which seeks the lost – those who are viewed as being beyond the pale of the law books. God in Christ comes to those who in conventional social terms have by their very life-styles or life-situations forfeited any chance of fulfilling the law. Thus it is that Christ comes to give all people the real and ultimate experience of God as loving Father. (And this is indeed much more than any sentimental, subjective liberalism). The Creator is no longer to be pre-dominantly seen as a kind of stern, despotic sultan who only rewards those who are supposedly morally good enough. The Creator is, as a loving and caring Father, near to all his created beings.

What Christ has therefore by his incarnation added to the conception and understanding of God is that the latter, as loving Father is concerned not just about the collective future of a nation, a people collectively known as Israelites, but in reality deeply concerned about each and every *individual* (with all their various human needs) who form Israel and indeed, any other nation or race. Many of Jesus' sayings beautifully illustrate the depth and comprehensiveness of God's intimate love for his human creation.(9) It is of course clear that Christ's earthly ministry was firstly aimed at giving his own nation – Israel – a last, unique chance, as the Chosen People, to repent and accept the final and most perfect messenger with his message from the Father. To the Canaanite woman's persistent demands for the healing of her daughter, Christ at first answers: "...I was sent only to the lost sheep of Israel"(10).

But nonetheless, because of the woman's great faith in him, Christ heals the daughter. And the obvious lesson here is that wherever there is the receptivity of faith to Christ and his message, there the Kingdom of God will be able to take root and start to establish itself (albeit, imperfectly this side of Heaven). In the sense that the Canaanite woman was a Gentile – not a member of the Chosen Race – she could be said to be a "lost" person. Yet it is she who comes to Jesus, addressing him as: "Lord, Son of David" (11), demonstrating in those words an affirmation of Christ's authority that many of his own learned countrymen would not grant.

"For the Son of Man came to seek and to save what was lost" declares Christ (12), It is significant that in this Lucan version of the synoptic saying, "lost" has no Judaic specification attached to it. However, the important overall truth which emerges here is that Christ's outreach of ministry is aimed not at those who are the leading Judaic religious figures and experts, but rather at those Jews (and Gentiles) who are deemed not to be of any account in religious matters. And such people of no apparent account are 'the lost'.

The striking paradox here is that, contrary to the socially received Judaic opinion, God is often far closer to those perceived as being "lost"; to those who are in so many cases somehow enmeshed in an almost determinist life of sin and shame. (And of course it may not necessarily be their own fault that they are in such ongoing situations). Ironically, it is these 'lost' people who are more inclined to listen to and indeed welcome the liberating gospel of good news. Therefore Christ chides his self-righteous interrogators:

> "...I tell you the truth, the tax collectors and the prostitutes are entering the kingdom of God ahead

of you. For John came to you to show you the way of righteousness, and you did not believe him, but the tax collectors and the prostitutes did. And even after you saw this, you did not repent and believe him". (13)

The truth is, that with God, "lost" is only a relative term. For the Jewish authorities and prestigious religious groups such as the Pharisees "lost" tended to be an absolute term when applied to harlots, tax collectors and Gentiles. But with God, as demonstrated by Christ's ministry (and particularly by the parables already cited), there was no-one too lost not to be reclaimed again. This great truth can be fully confirmed by the fact that the only way Christ could enter into the world of human flesh and blood was to forfeit – or lose – his full co-equality with the Father:

> "Who being in very nature God, did not consider equality with God something to be grasped, but made himself nothing, taking the very nature of a servant, being made in human likeness. And being found in appearance as a man, he humbled himself and became obedient to death – even death on a cross!"(14)

Being "nothing" and a "servant" are in ancient Judaic terms equivalent to being among the "lost" – those of no account – rather than those who are perceived as the greatly religious and righteous. But what is most amazing is that the Father should subject himself, through his Son to the risk of absolute goodness being exposed to all the evils, vicissitudes, temptations and agonies of human life. Worst of all is the risk that absolute goodness in its outflow of unconditional love should be misunderstood and indeed, even spurned:

> "He was in the world, and though the world was made through him, the world did not recognise him. He came to that which was his own, but his own did not receive him". (15)

How could it be that "his own" – God's chosen people – did not recognise the Messiah when he dwelt among them in flesh and blood? The love of God is posited on the free choice to respond or not to respond to it. This was and is always the case from the *Old Testament* onwards. The authentic *agape* love is based on the risk that it may be rejected, for such love as St. Paul says "is patient...kind...it does not boast, it is not proud...it is not self-seeking"(16). Therefore it can only offer itself to be accepted or rejected; it cannot and will not force itself upon the other. The rejection of such sacrificial love is evinced even before the physical birth of Christ. There was no room for him at the inn.

Christ, by his humble entry into human life via a manger, comes into the world as an outcast – already he is in the category of a socially 'lost' person. Soon he will also be an infant refugee, escaping into Egypt with his mother and father from the jealous wrath of King Herod. And later as a young man who has left the security of family and home, now burdened with the enormously exacting and draining task of his itinerant ministry, Christ will say with perhaps some weariness:

> "...Foxes have holes and birds of the air have nests, but the Son of Man has no place to lay his head". (17)

Christ is the outsider. He entered the world as an outsider. His ministry is that of the outsider and his life is that of the outsider. But it is he who is the Son of God. It is he who is one with God; it is he who is nearer to God than all the self-righteous religious men of his time. In Christ, God reveals a radically new dimension: God is not some morally fastidious puritan. His concern with a person does not hinge on their moral status or social standing. God is now revealed, as pre-eminently a God who is always 'there' for his erring or falsely maligned creatures. Above all, God is a Father to the unconsidered, despised and rejected. As such, Christ's ministry is a radical transformation of the Judaic application of moral values, calling into question at the same time the mistaken extrapolations and values which had been made from the interpretation of and additions to the Mosaic law.

In many serious ways the religiosity of the foremost Judaic groups such as the Scribes, Pharisees and Sadducees, was flawed. It is true that many sects such as the above, as well as others like the Essenes and Hasidim, were profoundly scrupulous and committed in the performance of their religious duties. But had not John the Baptist lambasted the main religious groups (e.g. Pharisees and Sadducees) for in fact their failure, as he saw it, to "produce good fruit"(18). For what was at issue was not the outward show, the punctuality of worship and attention to ritual; such groups were in reality contributing no concrete actions of goodness into the wider community. Moreover, as John scathingly remarks they were assuming a false security in living off the credit of being Abraham's true descendents.(19) Jesus, himself, reserved much of his anger for such groups, precisely because as setting themselves up as the leaders and models of Judaic religiosity, they were actually opposing themselves to the true, undemonstrative and humble *agape* love of God.(20) Thus Christ attacks the Pharisees and allied sects for their hypocrisy, empty rhetoric and materialism. Such pious groups were guilty of mistaking the literalism of the outward show of religious ritual for the true inward spirituality of religion. As always, Christ was looking at the real inner springs of motive and the actual state of the human heart. In answer to criticism that he had broken the law of the Sabbath day by giving healing, Christ had sharply warned his critics to: "Stop judging by mere appearances" (21). Such groups as the Pharisees were by their outward protestations and displays of worship in reality seeking their own pre-eminence in society. As in the Baptist's criticism, the fruit they produced was not in keeping with a true Godly righteousness:

> "...for they do not practise what they preach. They tie up heavy loads and put them on men's shoulders, but they themselves are not willing to lift a finger to move them". (22).

The Pharisees are armchair theorists when it comes to the practical outreaching reality of Godly love. Moreover, they have, by their false ritualistic example and emphasis on the need for fulfilling all the endlessly complicated stipulations of the law, "shut the kingdom of heaven in men's faces" (23). The Pharisees, themselves, bear the heavy burden of discouraging their fellow citizens from any hope that they have of entering God's Kingdom.

If groups like the Pharisees really understood about the essence of religious faith, they would have understood the Psalmist when he declares:

> "The sacrifices of God are a broken spirit; a broken and contrite heart". (24)

For this is precisely the essence of *agape,* Christian love. But in failing to understand this how then could the Pharisees understand Jesus when he makes this principle of spiritual brokenness – submission, humility, meekness – the very condition of entry into the Kingdom of Heaven?(25) Being "poor in spirit" is the exact opposite to the glowing feelings of self-importance and social approval which the Pharisees are so often guilty of evincing.(26) The revolution of Christ, which in one important sense is the fulfilment of the law rather than its abolishment, is also paradoxically about transcending the ostentatious and legalistic righteousness of those who are the leading lights in practising the law. (27) In the latter sense, Christ comes to turn everything upside down. The radical newness of the gospel resides in that it works from inside outwards rather than *vice-versa*. This is demonstrated by Christ's severe rebuke to a Pharisee:

> "...you Pharisees clean the outside of the cup and dish, but inside you are full of greed and wickedness. You foolish people! Did not the one who made the outside make the inside also? But give what is inside the dish to the poor, and everything will be clean for you". (28)

If one neglects the "inside" one neglects the state of one's true, God-given religiosity. For mere outward ostentation and dutiful fulfilment of rules and regulations does not feed the growth of the inner, spiritual nature. But the "cup" will be truly clean if one operates from this inner centre of "being"; for it is precisely this inner centre which if fed and made alive by faith, that reflects the divine image (albeit a fractured image) in which all men, women and children possess as created beings. And the proof of the pudding, so to speak, is that when one acts from this spiritual centre there will be a practical outflow of Godly-inspired love which is beneficial to fellow human beings. Thus, for example, those in need like the poor will find instead of empty rhetoric and indifference, the genuine flow of love in its practical, helping and healing modes. As such this is a true manifestation of materialism, re-humanized, re-claimed through a resurrected spirituality.

The revolution which Christ came to accomplish in his life, ministry, death and resurrection, was as far removed as possible from the false secular materialism of mammon, for it was a revolution concerned to re-unify materialism with the deepest spiritual source of 'being'. That is to say, the radical, salvation project of the Incarnation is none other than the resacramentalization of humanness. While it is manifestly true that Jesus Christ was not a revolutionary rebel in the acknowledged sense of such a term, it is equally indubitable that the Saviour was not a conformist. Reading attentively through the gospel accounts one cannot fail to see that at every step Jesus was upsetting the received opinions of the various stratas of Jewish authority such as the Priests, Scribes, Pharisees and Sadducees. Christ was not fermenting rebellion but he was sowing the seeds of radically new ways of dealing with the perennial problem of existential relationship living. To rebel is to desire fervently an alternative to the currently existing situation. However, Christ, the Messiah, came to bring about change, but not in any direct socio-political, interventionist sense:

> "Give to Caesar what is Caesar's, and to God what is God's" (29)

The divine project is the *spiritual reformation* of humankind. With the arrival of Jesus – in human flesh and blood – there also is the manifestation of the Kingdom of Heaven. In Christ, who is filled with the Spirit beyond measure (30), the Kingdom is a *present reality*. Christ *is* the *way*, the entrance into the Kingdom, and in his own being he represents its fullness, its plenitude of life. The Son of Man does not then have to desperately desire like a rebel an overthrow of the existing socio-political situation, for in the spiritual sense He *is* the new situation. Christ exemplifies to the uttermost the Kingdom of God in all its divine characteristics. The Incarnation, itself, is the bloodless, spiritual revolution which obviates any need for physical and geographically located rebellion. And it is entirely in keeping that when Christ is confronted with the soldiers come to arrest him, that his policy is non-resistance and he rebukes Peter for drawing a sword:

"all who draw the sword will die by the sword". (31)

These are hardly the words of the Zealot liberator. But Jesus' aim had never been to kick Rome in the teeth, and one can perhaps understand why Judas, who *was* a Zealot, had lost his faith in his leader.

The salient feature in Christ's dealings and relationships with those he came into contact with (such as publicans, harlots and other despised or social outcast figures) was an *acceptance* rather than rejection. That is to say, Christ did not condemn sinners, rather his declared purpose was to *un-condemn* them, and he effected this by accepting them as human beings by demonstrating a Godly love of radical forgiveness. Here there was no programme of social rehabilitation but rather a setting free through forgiveness which allowed the sinner to make of his or her own accord the fundamental *inner changes* necessary to move into a better way of living life. And to accept people in the sense of not desiring to somehow remould their personalities or vocations is, if anything, more a strange blend of conservatism and liberalism rather than that of the revolutionist. Christ was indeed far from a prototype revolutionary socialist, who merely aimed to condemn the corrupt wielders of power for what they were. His revolution was concerned with awakening God's Spirit within the human heart.

In conventional ancient wisdom (whether Jewish or Gentile) a God is all powerful and cannot put himself in jeopardy by anything he does. In the Greek sense, Gods such as Zeus often entered the human arena, but this was not at any great personal risk, for they came in their own strength and resourcefulness as Gods, which obviously gave them immense advantages over the humans they came into contact with. In the Jewish sense, there were popular expectations of a coming Messiah – a strong leader of Davidic lineage – who would lead his people to a restoration of Judaic supremacy, but there was no thought that God, himself, would enter through human birth into the world. This would be seen as both unthinkable and impossible for Jehovah to contaminate his unity and glory by entering the world in human weakness as a baby. The true conception of risk in the minds of Jesus' fellow Jewish contemporaries was the project of overthrowing the Roman oppression. For in the Jewish mind this could only be achieved by rebellion and particularly under the aegis of their conception of the mighty, Davidic Saviour. There would be the risk of bloodshed, as in any time and space human rebellious conflict, but the successful outcome would at least be assured by the conquering, almighty power of the Messiah who would lead in battle God's chosen people. The *Exodus* had been risky but with the all powerful Jehovah on their side, Moses and the fleeing Israelites had seen the waters of the Red Sea close upon and annihilate their hated Egyptian oppressors. Surely, with the true Messiah some equivalent victory would be experienced against the Roman occupation. But a victory which was *spiritual* and therefore non-territorial was something Jesus' Israelite contemporaries could not conceive of. Their idea of the 'Kingdom' was physical; the 'Kingdom' was the land of Israel, with its centre: Jerusalem. The 'Kingdom' was geographical, materialistic, it involved land, prosperity and triumph over the Gentile enemies. It was thus conceived in human terms of *measurability*. The following lines from Psalm 2, express this typical line of Messianic approach:

> "Ask of me, and I will make the nations your inheritance, the ends of the earth your possession. You will rule them with an iron sceptre; you will dash them to pieces like pottery" (32)

Just as the Cross for the Jewish authorities was merely a physical sign of punishment for blasphemy, the idea of God incarnate in a carpenter's son from Nazareth could likewise be nothing other than blasphemous. For it was not just Christ's criticisms of the current religious *status quo*, his followers implied Messianic claims for him and the growing popularity of his charismatic and practical ministry that upset the Jewish authorities but perhaps equally the fact that he seemed in no way to fit the bill in terms of the general conception of the coming all-powerful Messiah.

Nor did Christ fit the bill in terms of any prevalent apocalyptic expectation of how the longed-for Messiah might burst in upon the worldly scene. This other pre-eminently symbolic conception of how God might directly deliver his chosen people derived from the *Book of Daniel*, and arose from the prophet's vision:

> "there before me was one like a son of man, coming with the clouds of heaven. He approached the Ancient of Days and was led into his presence. He was given authority, glory and sovereign power; all peoples, nations and men of every language worshipped him. His dominion is an everlasting dominion that will not pass away, and his kingdom is one that will never be destroyed". (33)

This vision of "a son of man" coming down into the human arena in full awe-inspiring heavenly power has the rather theatrical equivalence of the *deus ex machina* in ancient Greek tragedy, whereby the appropriate God would descend to sort everything out. Although here this is not exactly true, for in Daniel's vision, before the mysterious arrival of this "son of man", the "Ancient of Days" (God) has already judged, condemned and destroyed the great empires hostile to Israel and which are symbolically characterised as terrifying beasts.

But, as in the more human-based Davidic warrior conception, the point was that this human-looking, yet mysterious figure in receipt of immense God-given authority, signified and symbolized the conclusive victory of Israel over all her foreign oppressors. However, this "son of man" figure riding the clouds and coming from the divine sphere, is in his apocalyptic supernatural transcendence, an overleaping of the Davidic Messianic conception. The "son of man" figure does not function in the more conventional and particularised sense of a Davidic warrior-king, but constitutes rather a symbolic representation of the total dominion of God over all nations and peoples. Nevertheless, despite the positive sense of inclusiveness ("all peoples, nations worshipped him"), this "son of man" is conceived purely in terms of the apocalyptic immediacy of triumphant power. For such a supernatural figure who acts from "above," there can be no question of any personal cost or suffering.

To such four-square materialistic and apocalyptic notions of how the heavenly kingdom would be inaugurated, Christ's teaching was indeed radical:

> "...This is what the kingdom of God is like. A man scatters seed on the ground. Night and day, whether he sleeps or gets up, the seed sprouts and grows, though he does not know how. All by itself the soil produces corn – first the stalk, then the ear, then the full kernel in the ear". (34)

Clearly, there is mystery here; the mystery of the divine laws of creativity. The growth of a seed is secret and unseen, it is not susceptible to human laws of measurement. The Incarnation, itself, is something that happens secretly and unseen. There may have been witnesses to Mary's giving birth at Bethlehem, but the actual advent of God into human flesh is as mysterious and beyond human comprehension as the empty tomb and the risen Christ. Just as in the transformation of seeds into bountiful crops, so too the 'Kingdom' is ushered in by Christ who is seeded mysteriously by the Spirit in Mary's womb. And again, Christ must like a seed return into the ground in order to rise again and so manifest the victory he has won over the ultimate power of death. St. John's gospel recounts the words of Jesus spoken to his disciples only a few days before his impending death:

> "...The hour has come for the Son of Man to be glorified. I tell you the truth, unless an ear of wheat falls to the ground and dies, it remains only a single seed. But if it dies, it produces many seeds". (35)

The gospel of risk hinges on a vision concerning fullness of life – the "many seeds" – which arise paradoxically out of life's antithesis, death. The concept of death is thus central for the concept of the fullness of the 'new life': "...unless an ear of wheat falls to the ground and dies..." And to stake the new life on the complete, voluntary death of the old life – the old self – is as sweeping a risk that can be possibly taken. But the risk is internal to the individual, for we are not talking about new fullness of life via a programme of political or social reconstruction, rather, we are talking about a *spiritual reconstruction* within the individual. But if such a reconstruction be a real and authentic thing this is precisely where the risk will lie, for one will no longer be conformed to the world's likeness and therefore one will be at odds with all those who believe that the bread of materialism is all that matters.

The real scandal of theological liberalism is that it largely evades the whole issue of how materialism has not just corrupted western society, but also more or less destroyed belief in Christianity. In this context, the whole controversy of whether there is or not a God 'out there' is misplaced metaphysics, because if we are really to believe the gospels, we must accept the crucially important thing that God through Christ has broken into human flesh and revealed the present reality of the Kingdom. In this context, the debate on whether God is 'out there' is simply irrelevant. According to St. Mark's gospel, early on in his ministry, Jesus proclaims in Galilee:

> "The kingdom of God is near. Repent and believe the good news!" (36)

The kingdom is near because Jesus, the divine Son is here in flesh and blood and therefore *tangibly within* the world. Christ's assertion can only mean that through his own ministry and being in the world a radically new phrase concerning the revelation of God's kingdom is now ushered in. But the ultra-liberalist is not concerned with Christ as divine Son. For such a person Christ is not, as in St. Paul's memorable coinage:

> "...the image of the invisible God, the firstborn over all creation". (37)

Christ is rather reduced to a materialist level; he is considered only as an ethical figure from history. Of course, Bonhoeffer's "man for others" as taken up by theologians such as Gregor Smith and Bishop John Robinson, is a key strand of Christianity (38), and on one level it does represent a rebellion against the materialist ethos of narcissism. One can appreciate that the idea behind Bonhoeffer's phrase was the desire to re-emphasis

Christ the suffering servant in answer to an experience of a world in a crisis of materialism at its most evil. But the problem is unless this view of "the man for others" is properly balanced with the Pauline view that Christ is Lord of the universe, there is the imminent danger of going down a pathway which leads inextricably to mere humanistic altruism. (39) And to fall into that danger is to forget that God requires above all, a *direct worship* – to be loved for himself, not just through others. (40) Failure to realise this means giving Christ only half his proper identity; he becomes nothing *but* a suffering, social services servant; he is not the risen, triumphant Saviour, nor is he the Jesus, who when under arrest and questioned as to whether he was the Christ, boldly answered:

> "I am,"..."And you will see the Son of Man sitting at the right hand of the Mighty One and coming on the clouds of heaven" (41)

The quarrel is not with Bonhoeffer's re-emphasis of Christ's "being for others", but rather is it aimed against the danger of reducing Christ to a kind of dominating humanistic, Good Samaritan model, forgetting that neither the incarnated Messiah nor any Christian could be a Good Samaritan to others, apart from being connected by faith to the transcending power of God's grace. If God's grace is down-played we are heading back to a gospel where one is saved purely by good works.

Having once again emphasised the crucial point about needing to see the whole Christ ("perfect man, perfect God"), one then is able to go on to assert that the gospel of risk is ultimately revealed and illuminated by Christ's fulfilment of Isaiah's "suffering servant" prophecy. But even as Christ takes on this risk of acting in the apparent powerlessness of a sacrificial lamb, we must remember he takes it on not only as a sinless, suffering man but also as a God who has voluntarily declined his unlimited divine powers. Christ, at his arrest rebukes Peter for trying to defend him by the sword:

> "Do you think I cannot call on my Father, and he will at once put at my disposal more than twelve legions of angels?" (42)

Christ has *freely chosen* to be the suffering servant, but at any given time, should he so wish, Jesus could call on the whole might of Heaven to vanquish those who wish to do away with him. But that would not be fulfilling the purpose and goal of the Messiah's mission. Here we are confronted with the strangest of all paradoxes: that this glorious fulfilment of the divine purpose can only be realised through the vulnerability and weakness of the crucified Christ.

The human bravado idea of the great hero who subdues all his enemies in James Bond style is a million miles away from Christ, who defeated his enemies by sacrificially bearing the burden of their sins. Christ, who:

> "...was led like a lamb to the slaughter, and as a sheep before her shearers is silent, so he did not open his mouth". (43)

It is hardly heroic in the accepted human sense to bear the guilt and burden of other people's sins when one is oneself sinless. But this is taking the principle of the Good Samaritan story to its ultimate divine conclusion, whereby the entire human race is the victim of sin's guilt and shame, and Christ, himself, takes on the whole burden and responsibility of the situation. (Although, the cross has a cosmic significance which obviously far transcends the localised example of the Lucan story). But all along, Christ had affirmed to his disciples that his revolution was the complete opposite of human revolutions. First must be last in the sense that Christian heroism is bound up in being a servant unto others:

> "...the Son of Man did not come to be served but to serve..."(44)

And to make concrete that point, Christ gives the disciples that most intimate and telling example of humble service when he washes their feet (including presumably, Judas, the one who is to betray him), doing this within hours of his arrest. (45)

Christ's leading ideal of humbling oneself to serve others does not fit in with the ethos of a capitalist world which asserts that you have to push and shove to get where you want and to make anything at all out of your life. The Good Samaritan story is thus relegated to the realms of a pleasant Sunday school story. For in a society where people are too occupied with the trappings of mammon, what chance is there to know who is really one's neighbour, even if he or she lives next door? The risk of serving others and of therefore being a good

Samaritan, is the risk of being prepared to move alongside and into the other person's dimension. It is, the risk also of being rejected, even in the very proffer of help to the neighbour. Even paradoxically at the supreme and mysterious moment of Christ's taking into himself all human guilt and its shame, he is rejected to the *uttermost*. Even at the moment when Christ gives humankind (his collective neighbours) the saving help which only God can give, there is only rejection (or at best a mere uncomprehending despair in those loyal few at the foot of the cross). But such rejection was the risk God in Christ was prepared to take to open up the gates of reconciliation with humankind.

The Jesuit poet, Gerard Manley Hopkins asserted Christ to be "a hero all the world wants".(46) But one would need to modify Hopkins' statement to mean, " a hero all the world *would* want if they really knew who he was and is". For the tragic truth is, just as in Christ's own time, he is not the type of hero – reviled and nailed to a cross – that the world wants. People in their ignorance of Christianity, unconsciously ally themselves with ancient Greek belief that a God *cannot suffer*. It is the foolishness of the cross which is still, as ever, the main stumbling block. (47) The suffering servant, the powerless God, at the mercy of his enemies, is still something so embarrassingly pathetic and therefore ungraspable for most atheists and agnostics. Such people can only conceive of a God as a "being" (if he were to exist) who would be obliged to sort out everything "here and now". And because that is manifestly not the way the hidden God works, they refuse to believe in him. Conquering by the absorption of suffering rather than by a direct means of abolishing it is God's way of conquering in the gospel of risk. The cross, as Simone Weil has shown in her understanding, represents on a supernatural scale the transference of suffering from the "impure part" of man (the sinful Adam nature) to the pure spiritual part of man, which is supremely represented and magnified by the sinless, human Christ.(48) The only road to the transcendence of suffering and evil is the road of sacrificial service, where suffering and evil is endured rather than falsely evaded by the deluded sheltering in materialism. Materialism is de-creative because it is a false life-path; it denies that an authentic life is the living risk of reaching out from one's spirituality to give our neighbours the help, support and encouragement which they need.

To repeat, modern liberal theology's scandal is precisely its conformism and reactionary attitude to the false worldly materialism; there has been allowed a collusion between the values of consumerist complacency and spiritual contemplation and growth. In this the liberal's God has become a *laissez-faire*, free-market God, who in his extremely indulgent attitude is just as remote and irrelevant as Voltaire's deist God or Rousseau's clockmaker who merely starts up the universe. Liberalism espouses the freedom of the individual, but like fundamentalism it becomes conformist in happily tolerating a materialist *functional* view of humankind, which is in fact a denial of the individual in his or her God-given wholism. Both liberalism and fundamentalism reduce humankind to the false doctrine of materialistic self-fulfilment, whether that is achieved on the one hand by a cheap indulgent attitude to the sacred or on the other hand by a gross literal attitude to spiritual things. The truth is that in both the above 'isms, Christ's church can be perceived to be as all too similar to the world – just another type of club for like-minded people. And despite all the vehement denouncements of worldliness from fundamentalists, their self-centred vision of personal-holiness (which necessarily becomes a localised vision) does nothing to actually challenge the materialist attitude. But on the contrary, their double infatuation with biblical literalism and their own self-righteousness makes them fall into the same trap as those, who by coveting a false materialistic theology, blindly misunderstood and rejected Christ in his earthly ministry. Again, liberalism, with its almost paranoid concern of wanting religion to be acceptable to a world puffed up with brazen scientific *hubris* and technological self-infatuation, is willing to conform Christianity into something matching the likeness of such materialistic self-conceit.

When Jesus is arguing his Kingdom gospel with his fellow countrymen, it is precisely the attitude of materialistic literalism which is the problem. In answer to Christ's challenges concerning their hatred of him and his message, they fall back on a resolutely materialist approach:

> "Abraham is our father," they answered. "If you were Abraham's children" said Jesus, "then you would do the things Abraham did. As it is, you are determined to kill me, a man that has told you the truth that I heard from God. Abraham did not do such things. You are doing the things your own father does". (49)

The analogy with Abraham is crucial for both Jesus and his countrymen. The latter rest their argument on the literalism that they are the descendents of Abraham with the assumption that such genealogy is the ultimate insurance policy. (Such an assumption merely serves as an abiding excuse to cover up their real spiritual bankruptcy). But Christ is looking beyond the materialism of mere genealogy, for Abraham's greatness really resided in his spirituality – his faithfulness to the promises of God. If those compatriots debating were really the true *spiritual descendents* of Abraham, then they indeed would acknowledge Jesus and his message, just as their descendent Abraham acknowledged God and his great promises. But it is the blind materialist approach which blocks as always the recognition of God, who he is and what he wants from his created creatures. Christ's compatriots, because of their blindness are forfeiting their true spiritual inheritance as Abraham's children. Instead, because of their hatred of the Incarnate Christ and his gospel, they are "doing the things" their "own father does". Their own self-adopted father is the false father, Satan, "the father of lies"(50). Christ therefore is accusing his hostile compatriots of being guilty of abandoning their true spiritual heritage. Once that heritage is abandoned one serves the master of a false materialism. One is no longer fitted to be able to commune with God – for the simple reason that the capacity to hear and understand God's voice is grievously impaired. When at the conclusion of this reported exchange with his fellow Jews, Jesus boldly asserts: "before Abraham was born, I am!"(51), instead of the elicitation of a reverential acknowledgement, there is only engendered a destructive hatred.

The gospel of risk is thus, as we see it proclaimed and enacted by Christ, the denouncement of the self-assured materialist outlook and the re-elevation of true God-given spirituality. And while modern-day fundamentalists and liberalists fail to engage with the real problem of the usurpation of spirituality by worldly-materialism, much which passes superficially for Christianity will in fact be a lie. Christianity and affluent materialism do not mix. That is why Christ told the rich young man to sell everything he had (52), and why also the Saviour made the following categorical statement concerning materialism as a barrier to the Kingdom:

> "...it is easier for a camel to go through the eye of a needle than for a rich man to enter the kingdom of God". (53)

A person cannot serve mammon and God.(54) An over-concern with money and material objects does not mix with the worship of God, who is "Spirit". Christ risked being rejected and subjected to murder for his denouncement of the false materialistic basis of his contemporaries' practice of living and worship. However, one must once again repeat that Christ is not to be mistaken merely for some egalitarian, social reformer. What is at stake here is the soul of humankind – its very survival, through re-birth, re-generation of the spirit – rather than a programme of social reform. For the coveting of material possessions and money is only the outward sign of a disease which is fundamentally *inward*. Thus the real essence of materialism comprises a self-regarding attitude of heart which is opposed to the largess of true spirituality. The love of self and selfish ambition connotes the real interior meaning of a way of living which is diametrically opposed to the self-renunciation involved in serving others.

Today the authentic practice of Christianity is largely rejected in the west because it would mean serious interruption to a lifestyle dominated by expensive gadgets, which like computers and television, hold people thrall to a spurious, counterfeit reality. Without the development of the sciences there could have been no industrialised and technological "progress" or any corresponding advancement of materialisation for the increasing majority of people in the west. Science must be said to have an indirect but nevertheless major responsibility for western materialism. It is often asserted by Christian liberalists that science is a complimentary form of "how" knowledge compared to the "why" knowledge which is the special providence of "faith." But while this is true in a basic sense it obscures the fact of science's massive and transforming influence on humans and their world and how they think about it. It is claimed that science is neutral in that it is only concerned with discovering and enhancing knowledge of how living things (including humans) and natural objects function and exist. The examining and understanding of the workings or genesis of living and inanimate things must of course be necessarily undertaken on a materialistic basis. But how can science be considered neutral when it has been and still is the driving motor for momentous and radical changes in the modern and post-modern world? It is of course obviously true that science has in many ways changed things for the better, such as for example in improved sanitation, hygiene and medical treatment. But the developments arising from science's new discoveries and resulting techniques have paved the way for the mass production of materialist goods such as high-performance cars and various electronic gadgetry which tend to usurp the time, thoughts and energy of most people today. The argument that science is merely finding things out in a laboratory and that the real responsibility is with *those* who utilise such new or improved knowledge, is both naive and dangerously *laissez-faire*. Scientists have precisely a great responsibility because science is *not* neutral in its effects. Without the massive advances in the various branches of sciences, there would simply not be the degree of materialism which is rampant in the west (and increasingly in certain areas of other non-western countries). But moreover, science also brings into being a dominant cultural ethos. What, for instance, is Charles Dickens getting at in his portrayal of Gradgrind, with the latter's infamous demand: "In this life, we want nothing but Facts, Sir; nothing but Facts!"(55), other than spelling out (albeit, in a comically satirical way) the sheer ludicrousness, not to say inhumanity of a Victorian culture whose main ethos is based on using knowledge for greater productivity and which turns potentially creative people into utilitarian machines, thus ruining any chances of their attaining a deeper depth of fulfilment as human beings? Today, with the saturation of the various forms of technological "media" (impossible without the advances of science), people are bombarded with commercialism in its most coercive and vulgar forms. How is this neutral? Being, for instance, constantly subjected to materialism through advertising via the advanced technological media (the latter created by a form of scientific "progress", as was Caxton's printing press), is it any wonder that more and more people are becoming creatively undeveloped, thinking that materialism equals absolute reality?

Just as social philosophies such as nineteenth century utilitarianism are significantly responsible for creating the cold, sterile cultural climate depicted so witheringly in Dickens' *Hard Times*, so too, professional science from the advent of Darwinism in the second half of the nineteenth century onwards, has tended to create its own cultural milieu. Science in its usage may be neutral as a measuring tool, but beyond that its effects for the formation of new ideas, new theories (i.e. "the big bang") new outlooks and influences are almost endless. Something which can yield so much popular influence can hardly be said to be neutral. And whether the majority of people really understand all the technicalities of science is not the point, for the former are nevertheless permeated consciously and unconsciously by the industrial and technological products, techniques, ideas and values which ultimately arise from science. And like utilitarianism, science has its own, albeit more advanced and sophisticated, Gradgrinds, in such popularisers ranging from the late Sir Julian Huxley to the contemporary Professor of Public Understanding for Science, Richard Dawkins. There are also other brilliant and influential Gradgrinds in adjacent fields, such as Sigmund Freud, who always considered his psychoanalytic work to be akin to scientific work and who categorically informs us:

"...an illusion it would be to suppose that what science cannot give us we can get elsewhere". (56)

And this comment written in 1927 still constitutes the overriding dogmatic assumption of the post-modern, materialistic age. The assumptions arising from the scientific outlook (even granted that Freud, for instance, had a highly developed aesthetic sense) tend to as a general rule automatically bolster up and underline the materialistic basis of life. But "man does not live on bread alone"(57) and the challenge of Christ's gospel of risk in today's mechanical and functional age is to re-assert the absolute primacy of Christ-spirituality (as opposed to spurious "New Age" spirituality) over the emptiness of science's gospel of the unlimited progress of knowledge and human betterment – and thus, materialism.

In Christ's time military victory over the Romans would have done nothing to help establish God's Spiritual Kingdom; the Judaic idea of coupling the Kingdom with military success was merely a false materialistic notion. When we come to our own post-modern situation it must similarly be recognised that even changing to committed egalitarian governments would do nothing to greatly modify or halt the rampant affluence of today's western countries. The real transforming gospel of spiritual power resides in a Christianity which stands up against such affluence (which needless to say is always built on the exploitation and exclusion of fellow human beings) and points to the spiritual *agape* love which really reaches out and communicates to others. Such deep and meaningful communication (as opposed to the triviality of the media's adverts, films and soap-operas) is the ultimate reality of the universe, and on it is built the whole basis of God's creation and its creative sustainment. The world of Christ's authentic gospel is the world where the materialist barriers, which divide and alienate human beings from one another, are to be cast down; it is a world – a Kingdom, rather – where people are no longer to be seen as functional "things" or "machines", but instead to be seen as *unique, communicating souls*.

The scandal of a corrupt world, whose ethos is scientific progress and economic wealth at any price, is that it cannot and never can accept Christ's alternative "Way" of real human communication based on divine love. For such an alternative would destroy all the marvellous illusions of self-sufficiency and independence with which western man and woman clothe themselves so to carry on in the insane and relentless pursuit of materialism with all its greed, *hubris* and superficiality.

CONCLUSION

RISK, GROWTH AND MATURITY

People always want utopia of one brand or another. For Christ's contemporaries it was the re-establishment of the political and economic hegemony of Israel; in short, a new golden age of supremacy which was to be in fact everlasting. And today in the western world utopia is consciously or unconsciously still on the agenda. But as always it is something which is merely in conformity to the self-centred desires of those who envisage it. Utopia for the liberal is absolute self-autonomy and for the fundamentalist it resides in absolute similarity, where everyone takes the same "party line". Neither of these conformist utopias will do. Life of the Kingdom of God is at once more than unfettered human autonomy and supine, simplistic doctrinal agreement, for the principle of the spiritual life is *growth in obedience to the love of Christ*. Such spiritual growth requires a controlling factor which is anathema to the liberal's idea of liberty. At the same time it also constitutes a freedom of expansion in terms of attaining a deeper grasp of reality through moving forwards in a maturity which gradually sloughs off all that is restrictive and false in thinking such as second-hand opinions and prejudices. Such a comprehensive freeing is at odds with the fearfully controlled ethos of the fundamentalist. The gospel of risk – Christ's radical gospel – is about just these two supposedly opposed things: obedience and freedom. Obedience is obedience to growth and this is effected by moving onwards in maturity of the Spirit to the new spiritual Jerusalem. Freedom comes as a by-product of the perseverance and discipline involved in that journey. One achieves freedom by being alive in Christ and thus being a new creation in the Spiritual Kingdom of the Father. Being 'in Christ' and being 'free' are synonymous. But to be alive in Christ and to be a new creation means discarding anything which hinders the objective of growing in grace. In Jesus' time, myopic interpretations of the Mosaic law, which ultimately detracted from the mirroring of God's loving and compassionate nature and falsely conceived Messianic expectations constituted the main hindrances that the Saviour faced in his ministry of proclaiming and establishing God's Kingdom.

The "Way" of Christ is not the way of attaining utopia; it is rather the way of attaining *reality*. It is a risky way, which requires a person first to lose all that is egoistic in his or her life before they truly gain their life back again in a far deeper and soul-satisfying way. It is a risky way because one has to give oneself completely to Christ to be as Oswald Chambers put it, his "love-slave"(1). This means losing the sort of self-control we are accustomed to and feel secure with. It means taking the narrow gate, the way which is not so comfortable, safe and easy.(2) It would perhaps be a difficult thing for a liberalist Christian to say to his or her agnostic or atheist friends: "Jesus Christ is my master – he is the absolute centre of my life". To say sincerely such a thing might well mean inviting derision and a loss of credibility. A fundamentalist would have no difficulty in making the above declaration to other Christians or agnostic friends, but he or she might have difficulty in following Christ's example of speaking out his gospel in the presence of those (like the Scribes, Sadducees and Pharisees) who are most likely to react in unsympathetic and openly hostile ways.

The core reason for why liberalism and fundamentalism are both enmeshed in their respective brands of conformism is to do with their lack of any real, working concept of Christian growth. The whole basis of baptism into Christ is that it is baptism into the death of the *natural self* and resurrection into the reality of Kingdom life in Christ. But this involves the twin risks of being open to radical change in one's perceptions and ordering of commitments. Such a new, enhanced openness makes one vulnerable to rejection and all the resultant suffering which flows from it. It is Christ who, in his radical openness, does what none of his contemporary religious teachers would do, as for example, ministering to the supposedly, socially-unclean lepers. But even with these ostracised and neglected people, in one reported case, he experiences the rejection of receiving no thanks from nine out of ten whom he had healed.(3) In another quite different gospel incident, Christ, perhaps with a rising sense of righteous exasperation, exclaims to a group of people (possibly comprising religious officials):

> "...you are ready to kill me, because you have no room for my word". (4)

The lepers may be allowed some possible excuse for not appreciating who Christ was, but the negative reaction Christ gets from those who purport to be religious experts is even more painful to him. Rejection, itself, is a form of killing, and so Christ's struggle and his true follower's struggle is ultimately that of life *versus* death and light *versus* darkness. Spiritual growth only arises out of the risk of openness to others, and Christ (nor his great disciples such as St. Paul and St. Peter) could never have grown in the spirit without being exposed to all that was not comfortable, safe and easy. At bottom, both the liberalist and fundamentalist Christian want to be comfortable in their respective worlds of self-autonomy and self-righteousness. (And we may well ask if ultimately there is any real great difference between these two self-enclosed worlds). Let us therefore look at what it means and what it costs to be committed to spiritual growth in Christ.

Biologically, we all start off as babies, but when we are born again as Christians (by the free gift of faith) we start off as spiritual babies. We are as yet undeveloped. The spiritual life has definite laws concerning growth, just as the natural world has its own definite laws of evolution. All growth, whether biological or spiritual, starts from the embryonic stage. The goal for each Christian is to develop into the spiritual fullness of Christ, the Saviour, just as the baby's goal is to grow into a fully realized adult. This analogy is in fact used tellingly by St. Peter:

> "Like newborn babies, crave pure spiritual milk, so that by it you may grow up in your salvation, now that you have tasted that the Lord is good". (5)

The problem with the fundamentalists is that they are so often prone to remaining merely at the babyhood stage of being a Christian. They evince all the boundless elation of their initial experience of salvation, but they do not ever seem to "grow up" in their salvation. Perhaps the liberal Christian's problem is a reversal of the fundamentalist's problem, for the former could be often criticised as trying to act like a grown-up Christian adult without having gone through the necessary stage of first being born a baby Christian!

Whereas biological growth happens on the whole without any conscious volition, spiritual growth *does* require conscious choice, even though the actual growth can only come through God's grace in the Holy Spirit. Although the completed achievement of growth into the spiritual fullness of Christ will only be finally realized on the other side of eternity, it is not enough for a Christian to remain a spiritually undeveloped baby. There is an overriding need to move from *childship* in Christ to *sonship* in Christ. What is it then, to be a growing Christian in the true sense of one who takes up his or her cross to follow Jesus? The answer has been well intimated by Henry Drummond, in his usage of the word "correspondence", which occurs in his book: *Natural Law in the Spiritual World* (6). Growth in grace can only come from being a *corresponding person*; in other words, a person willing to correspond in the spiritual environment with God the Father, and in the human environment to be a person willing to correspond positively with as many other people as possible – whether Christians or non-Christians. What I understand by the term "correspond", in its practical outworking sense, is simply the ability and commitment to both communicate sensitively, intelligently and compassionately with other people. Whenever we communicate to another person we *affect* them in one degree or another. Communication is a responsibility if one really takes it seriously. The task of the Christian is therefore to be a Christ-corresponding person, who is able as a result to correspond with the varying needs of as wide a range of people as possible. Such Christ-correspondence is a far deeper thing than merely chattering soothingly to whoever comes into our immediate field of vision. The challenge here is that we must start cultivating a process of *spiritual awareness* of the needs of others, which is to say, an enhanced apprehension of what might be their real core needs. But in order to achieve such a high goal of human interfacing, there must also be a parallel ongoing process of self re-orientation. We must bit by bit renounce the old Adam (lower nature) ways of communication in which we often communicate ourselves; such ways include being domineering, insensitive, impatient and manipulative. Needless to say, these modes of communication are hurtful to others and undermine or destroy relationships.

It is a disarmingly simple yet profound fact that:

> "...most of the difficulties of trying to live the Christian life arise from attempting to half-live it".
> (7)

St. Peter's point about "growing up in your salvation", and also elsewhere his exhortation to "grow in the grace and knowledge of our Lord and Saviour" (8), centres on exactly the above point made by Henry Drummond. There is a constant need for the Christian to live more fully the Christian life – not "half-live it". What is the result of this "growing up"? Surely it is a greater correspondence with God in Christ by communing with the realities of the spiritual environment, which needless to say include the "fruits of the Spirit".(9) This is the proof of the pudding in terms of being really set free in Jesus Christ. But "growing up in your salvation" is not the cheap gospel whereby there is no constant struggle, effort and even despair of spirit. It is not the easy gospel of the fundamentalist, who believes that one finds all the answers to life's problems tailor-made in the Bible. Nor is it the easy gospel of the liberal, who would rather maintain a detached attitude towards the challenging spiritual realities.

To "grow in grace" and "growing up in your salvation" can only occur if one is set free in Christ. But what is it to be set free in Christ? It is to have firstly experienced the inner awareness of judgement; that is, it is to recognise one's sinfulness in the eyes of the Creator. Secondly, it is to then experience God's gift of forgiveness through the redeeming love of Christ. Thus to be set free in Christ is to be in a new and right relation to God. One is set free from all the repressed and suppressed guilt and shame which was insidiously shackling and condemning us. To truly receive this freedom from Jesus is to be able to say with St. Paul:

> "Therefore, there is now no condemnation for those who are in Christ Jesus" (10)

However, the fundamentalist often wrongly assumes that one is comprehensively set free when one first accepts Christ into his or her life. There is of course a significant 'freeing' at such a first important stage in the Christian life, but it is only the start of a process (such as at the start of Christian's journey in *Pilgrim's Progress*), not a ready-made triumphal ending. Progress to real maturity in the Christian life is postulated on risk. There is no real achieved freedom without risk and Christian maturity is a result of *being free* in Christ and *using* that freedom to move into new challenging situations which require a deeper and more creative understanding of life. It is just precisely here that we see the fundamentalist fault line of triumphal joy in its inadequacy with respect to real Christian growth and maturity. It is inadequate because triumphal joy is only a partial reflection of the Christian life. To elevate a feeling of triumph and joy to the status of being the core Christian experience is to forget that even Christ was subject to all the frustrations and pain of the human condition; he wept over Jerusalem, he chided his disciples for their lack of faith and understanding; he experienced physical and mental exhaustion and on occasion vented his anger (albeit with a legitimate righteousness). Triumphal joy, when ossified into a set attitude, tends to overlook the cost of the cross, forgetting that the latter was itself the final evidence of Christ's supreme growth into maturity as the new archetypal bearer of 'purified humanness'. Such amazing growth could only paradoxically occur through the various sufferings of rejection which led finally to the total rejection at Calvary.

Liberalism, because of its innate caution and scepticism, also fails in terms of achieving real freedom in Christ. The liberal is rather like the cautious and fearful servant in Christ's Parable of the Talents. (11) The servant was fearful of the element of risk involved in investing his master's money in order to increase it, and so he buried his talent in the ground. The point of this parable surely dovetails with Jesus' saying (in the synoptic gospels) that he who tries to save his life (by rejecting the gospel) will lose it, but he who loses his life in Christ will in fact gain the new abundant salvation life.(12) One does not grow by being cocooned in an over-scrupulous desire for safety. To hide away one's positive abilities through cautiousness, is in effect, to restrict one's own freedom. It is to be unresponsive to the call of Christ and therefore the exact opposite of corresponding with the spiritual environment of the Kingdom. Again, one is reminded of Jesus' indictment of his fellow Israelites:

> "To what can I compare this generation? They are like children sitting in the market places and calling out to others:
> "We played the flute for you, and you did not dance; we sang a dirge, and you did not mourn". (13)

Caution and scepticism by their very nature rule out the

radical responsiveness which Christ's new order of creation absolutely demands. When we are faced with the gospel of Christ we are faced with a crisis of decision. There is no half-way house.

> "....if anyone is in Christ, he is a new creation, the old has gone, the new has come!" (14)

Either one is to be made new in Christ or one is to carry on as before in the old self. There is no room for the pains-taking logical steps of negotiation, for just as the advent of Christ in human history marked the absolutely unique breaking-in of God's Spirit into humanity, so too does Christ today and every single day face every man and woman with the opportunity of entering the new order of the spiritual environment. It is not a case of being persuaded by a logic of eloquent reasonings, but rather, as St. Paul puts it, because "Christ's love compels us"(15). The liberal attitude is by nature opposed to the urgency of compulsion. But not to make the choice of entering into the new creation is in itself to have made a choice by default. As Blaise Pascal says with regard to his celebrated wager argument:

> "...there is no room for hesitation, you must give everything. And thus since you are obliged to play, you must be renouncing reason if you hoard your life rather than risk it for an infinite gain..."(16)

But the critical choice we face in our life is no mere wager or game; it is for real. To hesitate is to lose the new creation of

Christ through the combined weakness of caution and scepticism.

In *Acts of the Apostles,* it is recounted how St. Paul witnessed to his own Jewish race in Ephesus:

> "Paul entered the synagogue and spoke boldly there for three months, arguing persuasively about the kingdom of God. But some of them became obstinate; they refused to believe and publicly maligned the Way. So Paul left them." (17)

Here, there was apparently no great success story. St. Paul had to engage in a persistent and protracted dialogue. There was no instant mass conversion and indeed after three months there were still some whom the apostle could not convince. Moreover, St. Paul experienced rejection as those who rejected his words "publicly maligned the Way". But this is the risk of preaching Christ's gospel. To preach to those who will only respond by humiliating you is a million miles away from the big orchestrated gatherings where celebrity evangelists speak in front of already convinced (or at least half-convinced) crowds. There is nothing spectacular or emotion-peaking in being rejected. But such rejection is paradoxically more a proof of the authentic Christian gospel (the theology of the cross) than the often superficial emotional assurance which emanates from big rallies (the theology of glory).

The lesson which seems to come out of St. Paul's missionary experiences (such as the above cited) is that there must be dialogue with those who are as yet outside the Church of Jesus Christ. The ability to accept rejection is essential to real Christian growth in maturity. It is just this fact which evidences that one is really free in Christ. If ever a man was coming close to total freedom in Jesus Christ, surely it was St. Paul. This is attested by his sheer willingness to go into difficult and often seemingly fruitless situations in order to persevere in the preaching and proclamation of Christ's gospel. The following is a remarkable self-summary of St. Paul's openness of application and adaptability to the challenge of spreading the gospel:

> "Though I am free and belong to no man, I make myself a slave to everyone, to win as many as possible. To the Jews I became like a Jew, to win the Jews. To those under the law I became like one under the law (though I myself am not under the law), so as to win those under the law. To those not having the law I became like one not having the law (though I am not free from God's law but am under Christ's law), so as to win those not having the law. To the weak I became weak, to win the weak. I have become all things to all men so that by all possible means I might save some. I do all this for the sake of the gospel, that I may share in its blessings". (18)

One cannot help but notice the paradox which is inherent in the above statement. Paul is "free" in Christ but he becomes "a slave to everyone" in terms of putting his own human needs entirely in a secondary place as opposed to the salvation needs of those who do not know Christ. Being free in Christ means here being free to put oneself potentially at risk by becoming "a slave to everyone". Freedom is not to be merely thought of as some sort of superior state of spirituality, but rather as freedom for practically acting out the 'new creation' life. It is something to be shared with everyone. The apparent accommodation to the varying socio-religious situations of Jews under the Mosaic law and Gentiles not under such a law, and to those who are "weak" ("weak" in poverty or spirit or in their Christian faith?), would seem to suggest an abrogation of Paul's Christian freedom, but in fact it merely instances the supreme *usage* of that freedom.

Accommodation in St. Paul's context means exhibiting a creative openness of attitude towards others and an acceptance of them in terms of who they are in their present 'life' situation. It is the perfect example of what it is to be an open-door, corresponding Christian, manifesting the non-rejectional approach of Christ, himself. St. Paul is in fact being Bonhoeffer's "man for others". But the Pauline sense of this phrase goes beyond the liberal humanistic emphasis on being a good neighbour; it extends to being a selfless and adaptable *witness* to the saving power of Christ's salvation gospel. Thus St. Paul, while being a "man for others", such as his Saviour was, does so without compromise to the gospel. There is no accommodating of any conflicting, non-Christian ideas. The gospel is thus maintained and in fact is proclaimed, but it is not done so in a prejudiced, strait-laced manner. It is proclaimed with rather a self-emptying (which in a humble way mirrors Christ's own self-emptying as he took on human flesh and blood) that allows Paul to creatively put himself on the same level as his hearer or hearers so that he becomes "all things to all men". There is also a humility here which is light years away from the arrogance of cock-sure celebrity preachers, for Paul does not say that he "becomes all things" in order that he will save everyone but rather that he "might save some". Furthermore, Paul's desire to help effect the salvation of others is based on the true democracy of the Holy Spirit, for he clearly recognises there can no longer be any room for particularism in terms of nationalism, racialism, sex and class:

> "There is neither Jew nor Greek, slave nor free, male nor female, for you are all one in Christ Jesus" (19).

Thus Paul writes in his letter to the Galatians, and in his missionary ministry this is the motivating belief and attitude which makes him so successful. (Incidentally, Paul's democratic openness of the spirit as evidenced above must surely explode the usual crude accusations levelled against him as being bigoted and sexist).

The only real adulthood is spiritual and real freedom in Christ is freedom from the blindness which causes a narrow and selfish perspective to emerge. The freedom of the Spirit that both Christ and his disciple Paul evinced enabled them to forget any concerns for their own comfort and well-being and instead to make it their primary aim to proclaim effectively the gospel of reconciliation and salvation. The need of the present time and for all times is the need for such a freedom in Christ, which allows Christians to forget their own comfortableness and instead concentrate on growing up in the Spirit by allowing the latter to let them enter more boldly and responsively into the needs of others. Dialogue as evidenced by St. Paul's experiences is debate; it is as much in his case being prepared to debate with legalistic Jews on their own level as well as being prepared to debate with Epicurean and Stoic philosophers on their wave-length. The supremely mature Christian is, while firmly established in Christ, flexible in terms of being able to adjust to the different life-situations of those who are being witnessed to.

True Christian maturity is posited on the gospel of risk. St. Paul complains to the Corinthians that they have still not reached the stage in Christian growth where they are ready for "solid food".[20] If "milk" is for building up the newly born Christian in his or her faith, then "solid food" must surely be connected with a higher development in terms of Christian growth and maturity. Christ, in some of his last great words to his disciples before he went to the cross, spoke of the coming role of the Holy Spirit:

> "But when he, the Spirit of truth, comes, he will guide you into all truth". [21]

However, it is hardly to be expected that even the most ardently committed and well-balanced followers of Christ would be guided into all areas of truth by one quick flash of revelation. Such a guidance into all the various realms and degrees of truth must rather be an ongoing process – in fact the process of sanctification as it is commonly known. It is by way of this long and perhaps never (this side of eternity) finished process that a righteousness of true maturity is built up as opposed to the elementary truths which are fed into the new born Christian believer. The writer of *Hebrews*, complains to his readers that they are still only at the "milk stage":

> "Anyone who lives on milk, being still an infant, is not acquainted with the teaching about righteousness. But solid food is for the mature, who by constant use have trained themselves to distinguish good from evil. Therefore, let us leave the elementary teachings about Christ and go on to maturity"... (22)

The entry into Christian faith does not come gift-wrapped with tailor-made righteousness, for although in one crucial judicial sense the Christian's righteousness is imputed to him or her through the righteousness of Christ, in another sense (sanctification), righteousness has to be spiritually imbibed and learnt and this necessitates a radical re-orientation of the motives, values and attitudes which operate in the human mind and heart. If one is still living on "milk" it is clear (at least to the writer of *Hebrews)* that this radical process of spiritual evolution is not getting underway. And it will clearly not do to say that it is up to the Holy Spirit to effect all this work of growth and learning. For we note that the mature have developed to the higher stage of *taking* "solid food", because they constantly "trained themselves to distinguish good from evil". Perhaps the most signal and mystifying failure of many who call themselves Christian is precisely the failure "to distinguish good from evil". But how can this possibly be?

How is it that the history of Christianity has been full of such things as the Crusades, the Inquisition, abuse of papal and ecclesiastical power; constant punishment, torturing and burning of so-called 'heretics' (both Protestant and Catholic); psychologically damaging hell-fire preaching, and twentieth and twenty-first century extreme right-wing fundamentalism? How is it, also, that Protestant liberalism, although probably not guilty of a malicious persecuting mentality, has failed to see the sheer ungodliness of an unlicensed permissiveness, which makes human beings and their ever increasing materialism the measure for everything? The failure in each case is a failure of the attainment of Christian maturity. The failure is in each case a fundamental failure of spiritual perception, and what can be more fundamental a failure than to fail "to distinguish good from evil"? Again, one asks, how can this be? The *New Testament* and indeed, the *Old Testament* are both shot through and through with warnings about the pressing need to live a life which properly distinguishes between good and evil. There are, for instance innumerable examples found particularly in the Psalms and Proverbs:

"Let those who love the Lord hate evil" (23).

So exhorts the Psalmist, and St. John equally exhorts a certain friend, Gaius:

"...do not imitate what is evil but what is good" (24).

Both the Judaic and Christian religions are posited on the supreme goodness which is a central component of the awesome holiness of God. For the Creator is not morally neutral as many theological liberals would like to think:

> "And God said, "Let there be light", and there was light. God saw that the light was good, and he separated the light from the darkness". (25)

The light is good because it emanates out of God's own supreme moral goodness. It would be an absurd mistake to think of "good" here as merely a functional or aesthetic quality.

The opposition between light and dark runs through both *Testaments* of the *Bible,* and just as right at the start of Creation God divides light from darkness, there will be on Judgement Day a dividing of the sheep from the goats. (26) The problem of course is that it is easier said than done for God's people to recognise in every case what is evil. It is all too easy for inexperienced Christians or cock-sure fundamentalists to mistake forms of evil for the good. Perhaps Christ showed his recognition of this problem when he warned his disciples:

> "I am sending you out like sheep among wolves. Therefore be as shrewd as snakes and as innocent as doves". (27)

But to be shrewd, particularly in respect of detecting what is really evil requires some training and practice:

> "...solid food is for the mature, who by *constant use* have trained themselves to distinguish good from evil". (28, my italics).

It is only by the constant practical application of Christian spiritual values to specific social or political situations that the ability "to distinguish good from evil" can be built up. In this sense there is a need to "*do*" the gospel of Christ. There is a need to engage more openly in the problematic situations which arise in the various spheres of life. One learns nothing about the Christian life without some sort of engagement which transcends the merely theoretical. But real engagement means risk; it means striving to enter into the same mature spiritual outlook of Jesus Christ, himself. And that outlook informed by self-denial, includes being prepared to experience rejection and suffering:

> "My God, my God, why have you forsaken me?"(29)

Abandonment, dereliction. The cross is precisely in one sense rejection, the negative human outcome of risk-taking. Yet in another sense, the cross is the glorious, positive outcome of divine risk-taking: salvation. But neither the fundamentalist nor the liberal Protestant wants an engagement which makes them vulnerable. For in their different ways each is seduced by the love of power, whether it be the illusion of control achieved by a spurious self-righteousness or by a counterfeit spiritual self-sufficiency. But in the end the fundamentalist and liberalist both deny the power of the gospel by their respective demands for self-affirmation.

The gospel of risk is both about human vulnerability and overcoming that vulnerability by sharing in the new risen and transcendent life of Christ. The latter knew the weakness of his disciples, knew the risk that at his greatest hour of need for human support and companionship they would desert him. He forewarns them:

> "You will leave me all alone". (30)

Yet a few sentences later in St. John's gospel, Christ declares:

> "In this world you will have trouble. But take heart!
> I have overcome the world" (31).

"I have overcome the world". Jesus Christ makes this astonishing declaration on the eve of the cross, knowing full well what sort of shame and suffering awaits him at his arrest, subsequent interrogations and final agonies connected with crucifixion. The gospel of Christ is not a gospel which evades trouble, for it is pre-eminently the gospel of the cross. One does not, nor should one expect to escape the dross, pain and heartbreak of being-in-the-world. But as St. Paul says, echoing in his own way Christ's above cited words:

> "...thanks be to God! He gives us the victory through
> our Lord Jesus Christ". (32)

Paul was hardly the man in light of all his many sufferings (and self-acknowledged failings) to use glib triumphal expressions. Triumph comes only out of suffering, not by the latter being somehow bypassed. Whatever was Paul's "thorn in the flesh", his prayers for it to be taken away were not answered.(33) Instead, he grew even further in Christian maturity by sloughing off any residual pride, replacing it with increased humility and dependence on Christ. The only things now he will boast about are:

> "...my weaknesses, so that Christ's power may rest on me". (34)

Such words might Nietzsche have assigned to a craven, religious slave. But these words come out of an incredibly full and varied triumphal life; a man who was more than any other disciple of Christ responsible for the successful spread of Christianity into the (then known) world beyond Palestine.

> "For when I am weak, then I am strong" (35).

These are the paradoxical words of the gospel of risk. Here there can be no safety in fundamentalist authoritarian structures. Nor can there be any safety in the intellectual self-control of liberalism. The gospel of risk is a *letting go* of all the clever psychological mechanisms which human beings like to build up in order to create the illusion that they are really in control of life. But the paradox is that only by letting go does one become really strong and properly human in Christ. It is St. Paul's deliberate letting go of his own personal security interests and total engagement with the hostile or often at best, indifferent world of human sinfulness that so differentiates him from the self-cocooned attitudes of Christian fundamentalism and liberalism.

The gospel of risk is a gospel of continuing crisis, a gospel of continuing decision. But fundamentalism only sees crisis in terms of the initial choice of commitment to faith. Thus there is no real growth to maturity, but only rather a false sense of security. For once the initial decision has been made it is merely a question of always being joyful and thus maintaining a high level of faith. The sense of an ongoing crisis is lost. Theological liberalism sees crisis only in the sense that so-called "classical Christianity" is too restrictive of human self-autonomy. Growth is not spiritual, it is rather humanistic in the restricted sense of following deliberately self-orientated, rationalistic agendas. But such growth only ends up in another post-enlightenment blend of humanistic elitism and escapism. In short, intellectual isolationism rather than human solidarity. Christ's gospel, is however, about building a community of people who having being joined to his Spirit, can grow gradually but surely into a people who are able to live together in an advanced maturity of harmony and love. Growth of course involves risk and there is no real life without growth. But the real growth in becoming fully human (re-formed in the likeness of Christ) does not come out of men and women's own self-sufficiency. It does not arise out of human cleverness or merit; rather it arises out of obedience (meekness) to the secret and ongoing work of God's Holy Spirit. Thus the spiritual "seed sprouts and grows", but in human terms we have no real knowledge as to "how" this happens, for this process is not susceptible to rationalistic control mechanisms.(36) But as sons and daughters of Christ we are able to collaborate with the Creator, simply like obedient children *allowing* him to work through us by his Spirit.

The gospel of Christ is a perfect fusion of both power and weakness. Both fundamentalism and liberalism deny this fusion by each only concentrating on one half of the equation. Thus ensues the false dichotomy – in terms of the gospel and epistle records – between the theology of glory and the theology of the cross. (Looked at in another way, it is no more than a false opposition between God's transcendence and immanence in Jesus Christ). The weakness of the crucified, divine, yet human Christ and the power of the risen Christ (the latter who now exhibits power over the normal limitations of geographical space and material obstacles, while still manifesting himself in a recognisable human form and personality) both need to be held together otherwise a one-sided view of the Saviour ensues. Largely spurred on by Bonhoeffer's fragmentary but influential remarks (as we have already noted) a central strand of post-Second World War liberal theology has tended to focus on Christ's weakness perhaps consciously or unconsciously as a counter balance to the fundamentalist movement's huge concentration on Christ's power and glory. But the real final truth about Christ is summed up by St. Paul:

> "For to be sure, he (Christ) was crucified in weakness, yet he lives by God's power" (37).

To think only of Christ as "crucified in weakness" invites the danger of thinking of him merely as an *historic* person. It can so easily lead to the heresy that Christ is not alive now; that he is not now living triumphantly "by God's power". Conversely, to think only of Christ in terms of glory and majesty is to veer towards the heresy of dismissing the incarnate Saviour, who shared all the weaknesses which are subject to flesh and blood.

It is surely part of the psychological fearfulness of the fundamentalist makeup that the "suffering servant" aspect of Christ tends to be largely ignored or played down. The fundamentalist would much rather buoy himself or herself up psychologically by focusing on the power, might and splendour of the risen "Lord of all"(38). By contrast, to contemplate the weakness of Christ in his broken body on the cross is something which a typical fundamentalist would perhaps find too risky and frightening. The fundamentalist suffers from a simplistic, dualistic misunderstanding of "power" and "weakness". Everything is reduced to a crass, either-or choice. But this fails lamentably to see how "power" and "weakness" almost inextricably interface (indeed, harmonize) in the incarnate Christ. Jesus suffers in the flesh but he *chooses* to submit himself into the hands of his enemies.(39) This voluntary act of choice in fact shows incredible power rather than weakness. The fundamentalist in their aversion to anything which equates weakness with Christ, would try to portray him as some all conquering supernatural giant. The real psychological failure here is precisely this aversion to weakness; as if by admitting Christ's human weakness, this would render him into a weak character lacking in courage! On the contrary, the weakness of Christ can only refer to his suffering; being heir to all the limitations affiliated to possessing human flesh and blood, the Saviour suffers rejection, homelessness, hunger, thirst, betrayal, denial and physical and mental abuse. But Christ's character with all its epic resolve, determined compassion, magisterial authority and composure under hostility is the polar opposite of weakness.

A failure to accept the incarnate Christ's sharing of human weakness is as bad as the liberalist failure to accept the transcendent power of the risen Jesus. The psychological fear of liberalism hinges on the suppressed thought that in the risen Jesus Christ, is displayed the ultimate proof that God is actually the supreme and ultimate power of the universe. At bottom liberal theology is strongly rooted to the Feuerbachian fallacy, that God is deduced out of human goodness and therefore God is merely a symbol for immanent qualities of goodness within the human psyche. But such a God is not a God but merely an extension of the post-enlightenment intellectual's mounting *hubris*. The liberal in his or her conscious or unconscious subsuming of God's transcendence into their own vaulted self-sufficiency and self-autonomy, also perhaps unwittingly embraces the fallacy of Auguste Comte's and the early 19th century Positivists' optimistic and pseudo-scientific creed of a new advanced humanity.

Fundamentalism cuts off vital opportunities for spiritual growth by a dismissal of the crucial need to accept the reality of human weakness and a corresponding failure to recognise Christ's identification with weakness through his suffering in the flesh. So, too, liberalism stunts its chances of growth by refusing to acknowledge the cosmic, universal power of the resurrection, which does precisely what human beings cannot do in effecting a new order in which reconciliation, peace, joy and salvation is possible. Moreover, the resurrection – the power of God in Christ – represents the triumph of the Creator *in all things*, not just the good but also the bad. God as revealed by Christ is not merely the true blueprint of humanity but also the blueprint of *all things,* yet because God is *other* than what he has created, he is transcendently outside or beyond them. Liberals are often happy to see Christ as immanent, but to fail to see Christ also as transcendent is to reduce him to the purely "within"; to diminish Jesus to merely being a symbol of all the inherently positive qualities which only need somehow to be encouraged and released out of human beings. The risen, transcendent Christ, however, is the answer to the otherwise eradicable weakness and insufficiency of lapsarian human beings. To admit the transcendent Christ one must admit human insufficiency and therefore own up to both the weakness and badness of human beings. However, psychologically, it is a hard thing for the liberal to allow God to be God, the *almighty active principle*. (For as the Creator, God is alone the all-sufficient One). Such a humbling realisation would free the liberal from the limitations of self-esteem and self-seeking, and allow him or her to start upon mature growth in Christ's gospel of risk. Until the liberal can accept the salutary twin gospel truths that all is impossible without God and nothing is impossible with God (40), he or she will remain deadlocked in as complacent a conformism as their fundamentalist opposites.

In an important sense both fundamentalist and liberalist

Protestant criticisms of each other contain much that is very true. Liberal Protestantism has lost the sense of Christianity as the revelation of salvation. Fundamentalist Protestantism has lost the sense of the richness, surprising variety and infinite depth of God's means of grace.

Yet the end result is the same for both these 'isms. Neither will ultimately accept the hegemony of God's grace as it really is in all its *otherness* of surprise, largess and confounding of human ways and prejudices. The instructive and warning words of Isaiah go begging:

> "...my thoughts are not your thoughts, neither are your ways my ways" declares the Lord. "As the heavens are higher than the earth, so are my ways higher than your ways and my thoughts than your thoughts" (41).

God comes in his own way to us which is at once beyond our thinking and reasoning. Liberal Protestantism, loaded (or perhaps one should say burdened) with all its inherited weight of "enlightenment rationality", cannot bring itself to really believe there is anything beyond the supposed goal of the optimum functioning of human reasoning. Neither can Protestant fundamentalism, in its lack of humility, really persuade itself that God's Spirit is capable of acting in manifold and diverse ways in order to meet the needs of each separate individual. In both cases there is rebellion, for it is God in Christ who is "the Way" not liberal or fundamentalist doctrines. The sharp rebuke to Peter is applicable:

> "You do not have in mind the things of God, but the things of men" (42).

For St. Peter could not accept the thought of Christ being put to death, and (at the particular time of his rebuke) could only envisage Christ as being successful by a concrete – possibly militaristic – triumph over his detractors. The gospel of risk, however, is concerned with having the same mind as Christ (43); that is, following his "Way" not human ways. And this is the real mark of Christian maturity: Does this person or that person, in making a response to a situation, really exhibit the mind of Christ, or are they only exhibiting a mind conformed and limited by various human attitudes? It may well be that much of the baggage carried by liberals and fundamentalists will need to be jettisoned in order to follow the "Way" of Christ and cultivate a conformity to his mind. Yet this is the biggest and strangest paradox of all: *conformity to Christ* is the essence of real growth and maturity. But because conformity to Christ it is at odds with the way of the world it also constitutes the gospel of risk.

Jesus was crucified because he forgave sinners. This is the great irony of the Christian faith. Because Jesus directed the love of God to those who were considered in social terms unforgivable and unloveable, he placed himself in direct opposition to the religious authorities of his day. The gospel message he brought was that men and women do not come to God through merit, through their degree of success in keeping the Mosaic law; rather, it is God, himself, who comes seeking his creatures, and particularly those who like the Prodigal Son, are considered lost and beyond hope. Christ enacts in his ministry this seeking initiative of the Father. Jesus goes out to such as the despised tax collectors and breaks bread with them in their own homes. Yet Christ became designated a public enemy because of this constant reaching out of healing and forgiving love. The maturity of Christ resides in his choosing to carry out his ministry in this way which would undoubtedly put him at risk from the jealous and ignorant hate of those in power. The tragedy of the gospel of risk is that God's surpassing desire to forgive and restore human beings from the guilt of their sins was so grossly misunderstood that his precious Son, Jesus Christ, was continually reviled and finally executed as a supposed blasphemer and enemy to the religious, social and political *status quo*. Why was Christ and his message not accepted? Those in power were intent on following their own ways. The "things of men" were more important than the "things of God". Forgiveness, reconciliation and restoration do not figure very largely in the human scale of things, for it is easier and certainly less risky to judge and condemn others than to squarely judge oneself. So it was in Jesus' time and so it is today. May it not be that despite their respective constructions of faith, many fundamentalists and liberals in the end find the reality of God's forgiveness in Christ too radical? Like many agnostics and even atheists, at bottom they want to be free of their numbing guilt, but when it comes to the realization that the "Way" of Christ is a "Way" whereby the acceptance of the forgiveness of Calvary must be chosen day by day, they baulk and turn back to the safety of their distorted, conformist adaptations of the gospel of risk and freedom.

> "Therefore, if anyone is in Christ, he is a new creation; the old has gone, the new has come!" (44)

So declares St. Paul. Either the phrase: "a new creation" is just a meaningless *cliche* or it is indeed symbolic of a life that is being revolutionized by being turned upside down and inside out. What is the reality of being "a new creation" in Christ? It is of course not a fully completed process of superior spirituality. But it is an awareness of being started upon a new radical process of liberating self-discovery and self-change. It is knowing that one no longer lives irrevocably locked in condemnation of accumulated past guilt. It is knowing that ultimately in Christ "we are more than conquerors" (45); that we can, through being spiritually united to Christ, overcome all the besetting trials and tribulations that are part and parcel of the human experience. It is knowing that despite everything that can befall us in life, we have a new strength and sustaining power incorporated into our innermost being. It is the knowledge that the very life of Christ is somehow by divine grace flowing within us:

> "I have been crucified with Christ and I no longer live, but Christ lives in me".(46)

This is the "new creation". To be sure, the gospel of risk is about crucifying the old self daily, because sanctification is a life-long process. Thus, in one sense, Christ has to be re-accepted by a daily prayer commitment into the believer's life. There is no room for complacency, for growth in the "fruits of the Spirit" – the achieving of a maturity in line with that of

Christ – is a massive goal which ought to absorb the whole of a Christian's human existence.

The gospel of risk is above all not about being involved in a project of spiritual self-conceit. Both Protestant fundamentalism and liberalism run the dangers of isolationism through their respective forms of spiritual self-complacency. Soren Kierkegaard warned that:

> ..."in the world of spirit the only people who are tricked are those who trick themselves". (47)

The perils of religious self-righteousness can only be avoided by growth into an all-embracing Christian maturity; for being "a new creation" in Christ displays itself finally in accepting one another (48). And to really be able to accept other human beings, with all their often infuriating, distorting and disabling weaknesses, requires a marshalling of the whole armoury of the matured spiritual fruit:

> "...love, joy, peace, patience, kindness, goodness, faithfulness, gentleness and self-control". (49)

The spiritual fruits, which generally accomplish their work unobtrusively, are not usually spectacular in worldly terms, but without them there is only their opposites: hatred, dejection, enmity, impatience, insensitivity, cruelty, disloyalty, hardness and self-anarchy. A world which does not conform to Christ's likeness can be ultimately nothing other than a mess. Such a world produced the cross on which Christ was crucified. Today, the nails are still driven in even by those in the churches who fail lamentably to move forward into a maturity beyond glittery externals. To achieve such fruit, for instance, as "patience, "kindness," "gentleness" and "self-control" means the gospel of risk. It means getting rid of our self-absorbing thoughts, prejudices, opinions and instead daring to become open with both oneself and others and thus espousing a charitable, non-judgemental attitude which builds rather than destroys bridges.

Christ could have had all the prejudices of his time against women, lepers, beggars, tax-collectors and gentiles, but instead we find he is gloriously free to meet each person without any pre-judgement. The cost involved was rendering himself vulnerable to rejection and misunderstanding. The cost is similarly the same today. Christian maturity is brought about only by the ongoing risk of receiving and accepting others, and until we move away from the crippling polarities of Protestant fundamentalism and liberalism, the Church of Christ will remain locked in self-regarding patterns of debilitating defensiveness. Neither fundamentalism or liberalism in themselves are capable of producing proper fruits of Christian maturity. Each 'ism by itself is incapable of producing the depth of growth needed, for each is locked into its own power-seeking agendas. The fundamentalist too often sees faith as if it were a supreme ethical value and consequently turns Christianity into a power-trip; the liberalist likewise errs in making God into a convenient abstract principle representing unlimited tolerance and self-autonomy. But the fruits of the Spirit are not the results of power-trips. They do not occur without a commitment to self-examination and the practice of self-discipline with its ultimate corollary of self-renunciation. A false Christianity is a superficial Christianity whereby conformity to Christ is never seriously undertaken. The qualities which really denote maturity in Christ, such as "patience," "kindness," "gentleness" and "self-control" are precisely those (unglamorous though they may be in worldly eyes) which help build and maintain relationships on firm ground.(50) When such fruits are really in evidence one can expect to find relationships which last despite all the trials and tribulations that no-one can ever be immune from. It is only when these spiritual fruits are in operation that life truly hangs together in a harmony which itself constitutes the proof that the love of Christ has gone deeply into a person and achieved radical changes.

A mature Christianity is about possessing or striving (with the aid of the Holy Spirit) to attain the *qualities of Christ*. The maturity of Christ is evidenced in the spiritual fruits he invariably displayed as he dealt with the whole gamut of human types: tax collectors, harlots, religious officials, disciples; the mentally and physically distressed, lepers, beggars and so on. Here, in the gospels is recorded the concrete practice of "love, joy, peace, patience, kindness, goodness, faithfulness, gentleness and self-control". In the end a truly mature Christianity is about the *actual practise* of the qualities of Christ and this in itself constitutes a liberating freedom which is in stark contrast to the fundamentalists stubbornly trying to live off the 'spiritual credit' of their conversion experiences and the liberals locked in their abstract world of intellectual casuistry.

What is urgently needed is to re-understand what "radical" actually means in Christian terms. Contemporary Christianity is suffering from, on the one hand, fundamentalism's neo-Judaic, materialistic distortion of power and on the other hand, suffering from liberalism's more subtle rationalistic cultism. Yet the truth is that being radical in the Christian sense has nothing to do with either great public shows of righteousness or with supposed superior modes of theological understanding:

> "Blessed are the poor in spirit, for theirs is the kingdom of heaven...Blessed are the meek, for they will inherit the earth". (51)

To be in this sense, "poor in spirit" and "meek" is necessarily to be at risk – to be the losers – in the secular world; it entails being the poor relations to those who live out their lives under the spotlights of worldly success. To conform to the "Way" of Christ means becoming a "suffering servant" with all the unpredictability, discomfort and vulnerability involved following such a pathway. This is the real core of radical Christian change, namely, the discarding, freeing-away from all the false security mechanisms of materialism such as prestige, social standing and secular success. The oxygen that Christianity always needs in order to survive must be constituted not of the self-conceit of triumphal or clever Christians but rather of the endurance, patience and humility of those who serve through thick and thin. It is this latter line of approach which produces a mature disciple of Christ. Christian maturity constitutes the achievement of the radical gospel. And the way to such an achievement is when one desires and learns to truly follow Christ, prepared to accept the risk of becoming vulnerable by putting the needs of others before self-needs. This is, then, what radical and mature Christianity is: *Self-denial*. However, such radical maturity, which is postulated upon the ripening of the spiritual fruits – the latter enabling one to relate to others in positive and self-sacrificing ways – does not occur without the ability to persevere amidst the constant pitfalls encountered in daily living. Touching upon this, St. James both warns and encourages in his epistle:

> "Perseverance must finish its work so that you may be mature and complete, not lacking anything". (52)

Without perseverance – even in the constant jaws of apparent failure – the spiritual fruit cannot be achieved. There is usually little glamour attached to the daily self-discipline involved in becoming mature in Christ and thus treading the path of humility and meekness. It is a pathway which eschews the prestige and footlights of secular materialism. And yet it is a pathway to the full and abundant Kingdom life, where no one will be "lacking anything".

Both fundamentalists and liberal Christians fail to free themselves from the things of the world and therefore they fail to change the world. For them it is always "business as usual"; the agendas of the secular world still loom large. As a result, the fundamentalists and liberals enfeeble Christianity by using it merely to project and amplify their own already fixed life-attitudes. However, to be kind and understanding to your difficult or tedious neighbour is not "business as usual"; it is in its way a significant achievement and it constitutes the proof of the pudding in a way that is entirely beyond protestations of faith (however fervent or eloquent) in church services or meetings. Likewise, bearing patiently with others and exercising self-control is at once worth far more in terms of practical impact than all the welter of liberal books, articles and spoken words about the need to make Christianity less supernatural, more relativistic and so forth. In the end it is not what one says at church services or meetings, lectures or in books which matters; it is rather, what one actually does in relation to others and how one does it which is of supreme importance.

What one does outwardly in relation to others is a net result of the way the 'inward being' is constituted in its complicated matrix of thoughts, motives, attitudes and emotions. Thus, the Psalmist, sensing this inner jungle of potential disorder and sin, pleads to God:

> "Forgive my hidden faults. Keep your servant also from wilful sins; may they not rule over me". (53)

The question of ultimate importance is: What does "rule over" us? Only a Christianity which is free from the rule of "hidden faults" and "wilful sins" is of any use to men and women. My contention here is that the final glaring failure of both fundamentalism and liberalism is that they signally fail to engage with Christ's project of turning the bad elements of human beings into good elements. In short, the whole point of the radical gospel has been missed; the central issue of how human beings are to act differently – to act in the maturity of Christ's risen spirit – in their interactions with one another, has been evaded. There can be no such change without a turning upside down of everything. A Christianity which does not do this is no real answer to anything. A Christianity which no longer surprises or shocks the complacency of the world is one devoid of the vital dimension of incarnate grace in all its surpassing risk-taking and barrier-breaking. To find and realise such a Christianity, one may indeed start with the positive aspects of either fundamentalism or liberalism, but that is only the very beginning of the journey.

FINIS

NOTES

Introduction

1. Matthew 16:24-25, *New International Version*, Hodder & Stoughton, London, 1980.
2. Phillips, J.B. *Making Men Whole*, Fontana, London, 1955, p.77.
3. Ecclesiastes 3:5, *New International Version*, Hodder & Stoughton, London, 1980.
4. John 10:10, *Ibid.*
5. John 1:10-11, *Ibid.*

1: Christian Fundamentalist Conformism

1. The five points cover "the verbal inerrancy of Scripture, the divinity of Jesus Christ, the Virgin Birth, a substitutionary theory of the Atonement, and the physical resurrection and bodily return of Christ". Livingstone, E.A. (Ed.), *The Concise Dictionary of the Christian Church*, Omega Books, London, 1988.
2. Hobbes, Thomas, *Leviathan*, *Classics of Western Philosophy*, (Ed. by Steven M. Cahn) Hackett Publishing Co., Indianapolis, 1977, Chapter XIII, p.365.
3. Matthew 25:14-30, *New International Version, Ibid.*
4. Matthew 10:39, *Ibid.*

5   Jay, Elisabeth (Ed.), *The Journals of John Wesley*, Oxford University Press, Oxford, 1987, pp.34-35.
6   John 8:2-11, *New International Version*, Ibid.
7   Leviticus 20:10, *Ibid*.
8   Luke 6:1-5; Matthew 12:1-8; Mark 2:23-28. *Ibid*.
9   cf. Luke 13:10-17; Matthew 12:9-14; Mark 3:1-6; John 7:23-24, *Ibid*.
10 cf. Matthew 8:2-4; Mark 1:40-44; Luke 5:12-14; Luke 17:12-19, *Ibid*.
11 Mark 2: 22, *Ibid*.
12 John 1:3, *Ibid*.
13 John 14:8, *Ibid*.
14 John 20:29, *Ibid*.
15 Unamuno, Miguel de. *The Agony of Christianity: And Essays on Faith*. tr. by A. Kerrigan, Routledge & Kegan Paul, London, 1974, p.10
16 John 20:28, *Ibid*.
17 Romans 12:2, *Ibid*.
18 John 6:35:37, *Ibid*.
19 Romans 5:8, *Ibid*.
20 1 John 4:10, *Ibid*.

2: Christian Liberal Conformism

1   John 18:37-38, *Ibid*.
2   John 14:6, *Ibid*.
3   Unamuno, Miguel de, *The Agony of Christianity: And other Essays*. *Ibid*. p.154.
4   cf. Fox, Alistair, *Thomas More: History and Providence*, Basil Blackwell, Oxford, 1982, pp.118-120.
5   John 6:37, *Ibid*.
6   1 Corinthians, 9:22, *Ibid*.
7   Matthew 7:1-2, *Ibid*.

8   Quoted in Fox, Alistair, *Thomas More: History and Providence* Basil Blackwell, Oxford, 1982, p.150.
9   Matthew 13:47-48, *Ibid.*
10 Matthew 13:45-46, *Ibid.*
11 Niebuhr, Reinhold, *The Self and the Dramas of History*, Charles Scribner' Sons, New York, 1955, p.110.
12 cf. Dostoyevsky, Fydor, *Notes from the Underground*, Penguin Classics, London, 1972.
13 John 8:7, *Ibid.*
14 Matthew 15:18-19, *Ibid.*
15 cf. Cupid, Don, *The Long-Legged Fly*, and other of his various works.
16 cf. for instance: Lampe, G.W.H., *The Atonement: Law and Love*, in: *Soundings*, ed. by A.R. Vidler, C.U.P., Cambridge 1962, pp.173-191.
17 Matthew 11:4-5, *Ibid.*

3: Failure of Fundamentalism and Liberalism

1   2 Corinthians 10:12-18
2   cf. the following among many examples: Isaiah 2:2-4; Isaiah 45:22; Isaiah 49:6; Isaiah 55:5; Isaiah 56:6-8; Jeremiah 16:19-21; Daniel 7:14; Zephaniah 3:9; Zechariah 14:9, *Ibid.*
3   Genesis 17:4, *Ibid.*
4   The reluctant prophet Jonah was himself angry that God had mercy on the people of the city of Nineveh. cf. Jonah 4, *Ibid.* Such prophecies as for instance, Isaiah 11:10: "In that day the Root of Jesse will stand as a banner for the peoples; the nations will rally to him..." were, one suspects, far too radical and advanced for the nationalistic and legalistic minds of most Jewish leaders and priests.
5   Romans 2:28-29, *Ibid.*
6   John 4:23-24, *Ibid.*
7   Mark 2:21-22. cf. Matthew 9:16-17; Luke 5:36-39

8   Acts 10:34-35, *Ibid*.
9   Romans 10:12, *Ibid*.
10 Luke 18:19, *Ibid*.
11 Matthew 25:31-46, *Ibid*.
12 See David Holbrook's: *Lost Bearings in English Poetry*, Vision Press, 1977, which is a useful study of the failure of Hughes and Larkin and other post-modern poets to write with any real degree of "creative sympathy".
13 Robinson, John: *Honest to God*, SCM Press, 1963.
14 cf. The BBC television series, *The Sea of Faith* and various articles, interviews as well as a plethora of books published by SCM Press.
15 Cupitt, Don, *The Long Legged Fly*, SCM Press, 1987, p.7
16 Rorty, Richard, *The Contingency of Language*, London Review of Books, 17th April, 1986. p.6
17 Rorty, Richard, *Ibid*. p.3
18 Cupitt, Don, *The Long Legged Fly*, SCM Press, 1987, Author's Note.
19 *Sermon No.20*, Yale edition of *The Works of Samuel Johnson*, Vol.XIV, edited by Hagstrum & Gray, New Haven, 1978, p.223.
20 cf. *Outline for a Book, Chapter 2*, Dietrich Bonhoeffer, *Selected Writings*, ed. by John de Gruchy, Collins, 1987, p.274.
21 Smith, Ronald Gregor, *The New Man*, SCM Press, 1956, p.101.
22 Colossians 1:16-17, *Ibid*.
23 Smith, Ronald Gregor, *The New Man*, SCM Press, 1956, p.67.
24 2 Corinthians 1:20, *Ibid*.
25 John 10:10, *Ibid*.
26 Colossians 3:3, *Ibid*.
27 John 3:1-21, *Ibid*.
28 2 Corinthians 5:17, *Ibid*.
29 cf: St. Paul: "... I no longer live, but Christ lives in me". Galatians:2:20, *Ibid*.
30 Luke 23:43, *Ibid*.
31 Lewis, C.S., *God in The Dock*, Collins, 1979, p.100.
32 See for instance: Sigmund Freud, *The Future of an Illusion* (1927)

and *Civilization and its Discontents* (1930).
33 Isaiah 6:5, *Ibid.*
34 Luke 18:13, *Ibid.*

4: The Gospel of Risk

1   1 John 5:19, *Ibid.*
2   Acts 4:12, *Ibid.*
3   Matthew 18:22, *The Holy Bible, Revised Standard Version*, 1971, O.U.P., Oxford.
4   Matthew 16:24; Mark 8:34; Luke 9:23. *New International Version, Ibid.*
5   Matthew 21:13, *Ibid.*
6   Romans 8:28, *Ibid.*
7   Luke 15:11-32, *Ibid.*
8   Luke 15:1-32, *Ibid.*
9   For example, the Creator's intimate understanding of human needs: cf. Matthew 6:28-32; Luke 12:27-30, *Ibid.*.
10 Matthew 15:24, *Ibid.*
11 Matthew 15:22, *Ibid.*
12 Luke 19:10, *Ibid.*
13 Matthew 21:31-32, *Ibid.*
14 Philippians 2:6-8, *Ibid.*
15 John 1:10-11, *Ibid.*
16 1 Corinthians 13:4-5, *Ibid.*
17 Luke 9:58, *Ibid.*
18 Luke 3:9; Matthew 3:7-8, *Ibid.*
19 Matthew 3:9-10.
20 Jesus teaches his disciples to pray in contradistinction to the method of such groups, cf. Matthew 6:5-8; likewise Jesus' teaching regarding fasting, cf. Matthew 6:16-18, *Ibid.*
21 John 7:24, *Ibid.*
22 Matthew 23:3-4, *Ibid.*

23 Matthew 23:13-14, *Ibid*.
24 Psalm 51:17, *Ibid*.
25 "Blessed are the poor in spirit, for theirs is the kingdom of heaven": Matthew 5:3, *Ibid*.
26 cf. Matthew 23:5-7, *Ibid*.
27 cf. Matthew 5:17-20, *Ibid*.
28 Luke 11:39-41
29 Matthew 22:21
30 cf. John the Baptist's saying: "...to him (Christ) God gives the Spirit without limit", John 3:34, *Ibid*.
31 Matthew 26:52, *Ibid*.
32 Psalm 2:8-9, *Ibid*.
33 Daniel 7:13-14, *Ibid*.
34 Mark 4:26-28, *Ibid*.
35 John 12:23-24, *Ibid*.
36 Mark 1:15, *Ibid*.
37 Colossians 1:15, *Ibid*.
38 See previous chapter, *Failure of Fundamentalism and Liberalism*, pp.71-77.
39 One cannot but feel that Bonhoeffer, because of his mature and deeply rooted Christian faith, would have avoided this danger.
40 Christ, himself, is recorded in the synoptic gospels (Matthew 22:34-40; Mark 12:28-31) as affirming that the commandment to: "Love the Lord your God with all your heart and with all your soul and with all your strength" (Deuteronomy 6:5), is the most important. Jesus ranks the commandment of Leviticus 19:18, ("...love your neighbour as yourself"), as being of next in importance.
41 Mark 14:62, *Ibid*.
42 Matthew 26:53, *Ibid*.
43 Isaiah 53:7, *Ibid*.
44 Matthew 20:28, *Ibid*.
45 John 13:1-17, *Ibid*.
46 Hopkins, Gerard Manley, *Sermon at Bedford Leigh*, 23rd November, 1879. From *Selected Prose* (ed. Gerald Roberts),

O.U.P. Oxford, 1980, p.84.
47 1 Corinthians 1:18-25, *Ibid.*
48 Weil, Simone, *Gateway to God*, Fontana, 1974, p.77.
49 John 8:39-41, *Ibid.*
50 John 8:44, *Ibid.*
51 John 8:58, *Ibid.*
52 Luke 18:18-23, *Ibid.*
53 Luke 18:25, *Ibid.*
54 Matthew 6:24; Luke 16:13, *Ibid.*
55 Dickens, Charles, *Hard Times*, Penguin, London, 1969, Ch.1, p.47.
56 Freud, Sigmund, *The Future of an Illusion*, trans. by James Strachey, Penguin Freud Library, Vol.12, London, 1985, p.241.
57 Deuteronomy 8:3, *New International Version, Ibid.*

Conclusion: Risk, Growth and Maturity

1 Chambers, Oswald, *My Utmost for His Highest*, Marshall, Morgan & Scott, London, 1972 (The phrase "love-slave" occurs in one of the daily readings).
2 cf. Matthew 7:13-14; Luke 13:24, *Ibid.*
3 Luke 17:11-19, *Ibid.*
4 John 8:37, *Ibid.*
5 1 Peter 2:2-3, *Ibid.*
6 Drummond, Henry, *Natural Law in the Spiritual World*, Hodder & Stoughton, London, 1898.
7 The remark by Drummond occurs somewhere in the above cited work.
8 2 Peter 3:18, *Ibid.*
9 cf. Galatians 5:22-23, *Ibid.*
10 Romans 8:1, *Ibid.*
11 Matthew 25:14-30, *Ibid.*
12 Matthew 10:39; 16:25; Mark 8:35; Luke 9:24, *Ibid.*

13 Matthew 11:16-17, *Ibid.*
14 2 Corinthians 5:17, *Ibid.*
15 2 Corinthians 5:14, *Ibid.*
16 Pascal, Blaise, *Pensees*, trans. by A.J. Krailsheimer, Penguin, London, 1966, p.151
17 Acts 19:8-9, *Ibid.*
18 1 Corinthians 9:19-23, *Ibid.*
19 Galatians 3:28, *Ibid.*
20 1 Corinthians 3:2, *Ibid.*
21 John 16:13, *Ibid.*
22 Hebrews 5:13-6:1, *Ibid.*
23 Psalm 97:10, *Ibid.*
24 3 John 11, *Ibid.*
25 Genesis 1: 3-4, *Ibid.*
26 Matthew 25:31-46, *Ibid.*
27 Matthew 10:16, *Ibid.*
28 Hebrews 5:14, *Ibid.*
29 Matthew 27:46, cf. Psalm 22:1, *Ibid.*
30 John 16:32, *Ibid.*
31 John 16:33, *Ibid.*
32 1 Corinthians 15:57, *Ibid.*
33 2 Corinthians 12:7-10, *Ibid.*
34 2 Corinthians 12:9, *Ibid.*
35 2 Corinthians 12:10, *Ibid.*
36 Mark 4:26-28, *Ibid.*
37 2 Corinthians 13:4, *Ibid.*
38 Acts 10:36, *Ibid.*
39 John 10:17-18. *Ibid.*
40 Matthew 19:26; Mark 10:27; Luke 18:27; Luke 1:37, *Ibid.*
41 Isaiah 55:8-9, *Ibid.*
42 Mark 8:33, cf. Matthew 16:23, *Ibid.*
43 Romans 12:2; 1 Corinthians 2:16, *Ibid.*
44 2 Corinthians 5:17, *Ibid.*
45 Romans 8:37, *Ibid*
46 Galatians 2:20, *Ibid.*

47 Kierkegaard, Soren, *Fear and Trembling*, trans. by Alistair Hannay, Penguin, London, 1985, p.125.
48 cf. St. Paul's exhortation: "Accept one another, then, just as Christ accepted you, in order to bring praise to God", Romans 15:7, *Ibid*.
49 Galatians 5:22-23, *Ibid*.
50 cf. 1 Corinthians 13:4-7, *Ibid*.
51 Matthew 5:3; 5:5, *Ibid*.
52 James 1:4, *Ibid*.
53 Psalm 19:12-13, *Ibid*.